Phil

Best Wishes!

Jeff

"I have known Dr. Jeff Magee for many years as an author, speaking colleague, and friend. Jeff is not only one of the leading voices in the field of performance, but he applies the principles he teaches in his own business. We live in a world where—when it's all said and done—there's a lot said and very little done. If you want to leave the talkers behind and start living your personal and professional life among the doers, I recommend Dr. Jeff Magee's *Performance Execution*."
*- Jim Stovall, president of the Narrative Television Network and author of **The Ultimate Gift***

"Jeff has nailed it in **Performance Execution**. He has just the right blend of powerful content, unequaled style and necessary truth. If you are ready to take action then you will get more from reading this one book then the last dozen in your literary library."
*- Lisa Nichols, professional speaker and author of **No Matter What***

"We endorse Jeff Magee's publications, because readers get practical immediate action. To prosper in the developing recession brains must move from the old economy into the new economy. Jeff leads with tips and "how to" exercises that compel the reader to action that makes the bottom line grow. There is no instant rice in making fortunes, outside Performance and Jeff Magee is the hot steamy water that swells that rice bowl to over flow everywhere in the Global Village. If you want a snack read the other guys. If you want a FEAST read Jeff Magee."
*- Berny Dohrmann & Mark Victor Hansen, co-authors of **Cash the Crash***

"My investment was designed to develop the leadership capabilities in each individual and you are achieving far more. In the first few months, the returns to the balance sheet are already evident. We are breaking sales records and growing our customer base. Personal initiative and accountability are at an all time high."
*- Rodney Sargent, CEO, **BancInsure***

"Your spirited and authoritative presentations captured the minds of our team and sent them home each month with a full box of new tools to use. These tools have already improved the target performance in many of the participants and their subordinates."
*- Alan Webb, Sr. Director of Training, **Taco Cabana***

"Once again, Dr. Magee has provided a pragmatic best practice guide for organizations to not only develop a strategic mission but insure that it is executed exceptionally. His words are inspiring but most of all, they provide clear guidance for exceptional execution of an organization's mission."
*- **Kathy Taylor**, Oklahoma Governor's Chief of Education, Strategy and Innovation; Former Oklahoma Secretary of Commerce and former Mayor of Tulsa, OK*

Performance Execution

Why Most People & Organizations *SUC* Today & Six Truths You Can Apply To Attain *SUCCESS* Now!

Performance Execution: Why Most People & Organizations SUC & Six Truths You Can
Apply To Attain SUCCESS Now
Dr. Jeffrey Magee

ISBN 978-0-9777957-1-0

Published in the United States by:
Performance Success Media Group / PSMG
and JEFF MAGEE INTERNATIONAL / JMI, Inc.
P.O. Box 70918
Tulsa, OK, 74170
www.JeffreyMagee.com

Cover Design: Stephen King
Book Design: Carlos Moreno
Editing: Joy Jones, Jennifer Moreno

Printed in the United States of America

Even though the distance between "Stimulus" and "Response" is only a nanosecond, it is a result of the "CHOICES" that you make…

Performance Execution© is about that distance we call CHOICE

stimulus – CHOICE – response

Table of Contents

Preface

PQ Reality Check: Your performance attainment is under attack today, and once you are armed with the prescription to counter the cancers impeding success, Performance Execution becomes second nature!

Who are you, and – a better question – who do you want to be?

We have created a planet on which individuals have learned how to provide minimum effort, yet demand maximum compensation. Environments have been allowed to manifest in which individuals have learned that someone will always enable their lack of performance and be compassionate for their destructive behavior. In this environment, Performance Execution in our personal lives and within our organizations is killed by the cancer of acceptance and tolerance toward people, who expect to be treated specially, despite never having accomplished nor contributed anything meaningful while on the planet!

The remedy is simple. Innovators do it, entrepreneurs live it, star athletes and performers are addicted to it, managers facilitate it, and leaders grasp it on every level of their lives… *Performance Execution*!

The world needs less talk and more transaction-oriented, performance-based, bottom-line, results-driven leaders – people who lead themselves as well as others!

Leaders have a **performance quotient (PQ)**! PQ is derived from a never-ending hunger to add to and challenge their **intelligence quotient (IQ)** to greater heights.

It is also derived from their ability to balance and draw upon their **emotional quotient (EQ)** in every level of their life.

It's Not Your IQ or EQ,
It Is IQ+EQ=PQ®

Your future health, well-being, and success will depend upon you acting as your own performance leader – kind of like You, Inc. The great Bill Cosby wrote about this in a column for *Professional Performance Magazine* (*www.ThePerformanceMagazine.com*) in Vol. 16 Issue 2, *"You Can Either be a Victim or a Victor,"* but either way, you make that performance choice (PQ)!

History does repeat itself, and history does not lie. As an award-winning journalist, performance coach and speaker, it never ceases to amaze me that in business and in life, when you surround yourself with greatness – and I mean true greatness based upon competency, credentials, and real-life experience – history reveals sustained and continued success.

$$IQ + EQ = PQ$$

There are six truths that I have identified which lead to individual and organizational effectiveness every time, and thus, overall success.

Conversely, when organizations or people surround themselves with victims, losers, whiners, and those who merely have lucky DNA (Trust Fund Babies), it is always vanity and negative emotions that guide your thought processes. This counters productive emotions and actions, with the net result being trauma in close company!

Performance Execution (PQ) is about how you can avoid the "suc-factor" in life by adhering to these six truths. Be careful, though, because reading this book will change who you are, how others see you, and your circle of influence in life. Truth be told, most people (and, sadly, a lot of organizations) prefer to "suc" and play victim. By reading, internalizing, and applying these six power principles, you will experience levels of success in life about which others would only dream. *Note: Don't be offended by the word "suc" because it is different than the word "suck." This idea will be developed further in Chapter Two.*

Some people choose to be good.
Some people choose to be great.

Only a few choose to be significant!
What do your choices reveal about you?
Newsflash: There is no SECRET to success!
Only ANSWERS!

And you only arrive at the answers by asking tough, inwardly-directed, logic-based, and not-emotionally-driven QUESTIONS. From these sound questions, the ANSWERS always emerge. Then, and only then, can you unlock your SECRET to success!

Successful leaders in any walk of life may not have answers, but they do have the innate ability (or have been mentored and trained) to ask provoking questions, which always lead to answers!

Have you ever noticed that there is no shortage of people and organizations that are envious of what others have or have accomplished? I have never seen a person or organization, however, which is envious of the work required to expand their gains!

We truly have created a performance expectation among individuals and organizations today, whereby mediocrity is seen as the benchmark of success, and those which reach the heights of "suc" are celebrated and rewarded. Those which strive to succeed are many times simply recognized with additional hurdles to impede their accomplishments. What is the basic difference between those which continually succeed and see success as their pathway for contributing their riches upon others and those which prefer to "suc"?

The answer is Performance Execution!

For the first time, two decades of research has revealed very clearly what super-achievers do and how they do it. This is how successful teachers teach, managers manage, leaders lead, mentors mentor, parents parent, neighbors neighbor, and how you can attain success and not "suc" in life!

It is no wonder that businesses like Southwest Airlines have, for 35 years, made money, provided their employees with some of the highest performance pay in the industry, and grown at a time when other major airlines continuously operated in bankruptcy mode or deficit spending. They can turn a plane in less than 20 minutes with three employees, while the industry norm takes upwards of a dozen employees nearly an hour.

It is no wonder that foreign auto nameplates have out-classed, out-maneuvered, out-priced, and out-produced Detroit on their home turf for two uncontested decades. Or how someone like Pastor Joel Osteen can create an atmosphere that brings more than 40,000 people every weekend to share in fellowship, while other spiritual leaders fight to even have an audience. Or how your sphere of influence either reveals a circle of successful achievers or individuals who prefer to "suc" as a way of life.

The answer is Performance Execution!

If you have made it this far, you must be interested in ways to attain higher levels of Performance Execution personally and professionally. You are also receptive to identifying the action plans necessary to ensure those around you reach the same heights.

In working with individuals at the top and bottom of a variety of organizations, it became clearer and clearer that those who achieved were doing things differently than those who were on the same payroll and struggling. I have worked with more military units and commanders across all fifty-four states and territories than any other civilian leadership performance consultant/coach in America for the past twenty years. I have also worked with the top Fortune 100 firms in America, leading government agencies, leading human resources soft-skill training firms, and more than 500 non-profit associations. >From these experiences, the difference between Performance Execution "suc" and success has become shockingly clear.

I have had a front row seat, working with and providing services to some of America's leading brands, including IBM, Pfizer, Boeing, Harley-Davidson, Anheuser-Busch, USA/NASA, Farm Credit Services, the Army National Guard, American Airlines/AMR, AICPA, and Southwest Airlines. These are not organizations with good or bad people. They are simply examples of how to engineer an organization in a way that allows people to be either good or bad. Some of these firms grasp and understand Performance Execution. Others go out of their way to ensure their own complacency and failure.

The answer to developing the critically important Human Capital strength within yourself and others, in order to attain greatness, is the ability to deliver Performance Execution!

One specific and vivid example comes to mind in the shaping of these models and the crafting of this book - my experience working with a well-known Fortune 100 company. I served as one of three outside training vendors authorized to help with the development of its field leadership sales force and executives, and I got to see first-hand how it rebuilt itself strategically and tactically to become the number-one-rated firm in America for which to work, three years in a row. I also had a front-row seat as I watched the company systematically unravel, and within four years of being rated the number-one Fortune 500 firm to work for in America, not even making the list of the top 100. This, in and of itself, would make a great case study on how to "suc," but in this firm's case, no one would understand it. And worse yet, no one in positions of responsibility cared to understand it. Some of their achievements under one CEO's three year tenure included:

1. Sales representatives with more than 5,000 years of total combined experience were purged from the company.

2. More than 75 percent of the learning enterprise team that birthed their nationally-acclaimed organizational infrastructure and national learning center left the company.

3. Their stock value plummeted.

4. The worst product launch in modern corporate history led the head of this colossal debacle to be elevated and put in charge of the organization's overall educational enterprise. Now that you quantifiably "suc," you can train everyone!

5. A climate of such extreme ethnic affirmative action was cultured in which those who had more than earned the right to be terminated were kept, promoted, and shuffled around the organization. Meanwhile, the organization's pool of talented players lined up viable new employers and exited through the back door as quickly as possible. Poor case of talent management!

6. The product deliverable crashed to such a low level that their client base laughed at the sight of them.

7. Legal backlash at questionable business policies, billings, and practices earned them daily headlines in world media.

The worst thing is that, in a day when people's vanity is so easily wounded, and we have become such a litigious society, people frequently sue for defamation (The truth hurts.). Instead of learning and growing, we regularly protect the incompetent and penalize the competent.

The answer is total lack of Performance Execution! When a person learns that he can use excuses for non-performance and people will still enable him, and give him that for which he has not worked, he learns that performance does not always matter!

People learn how to play the game and then consistently look for willing players to play in "their" game of life!

We won't even apply this to politicians, or we would have to purge the majority of them from our society. Isn't it always interesting how, in politics, the lack of Performance Execution is attributed to "the other guy" and never to the one speaking in front of us?

Understanding success on a personal level is also critical to understanding the mechanics of Performance Execution.

Serving as the Group Publisher of *Professional Performance Magazine* (*www. ThePerformanceMagazine.com*) for over a decade, I have had the honor of meeting, interviewing, studying, and acquiring powerful how-to themed editorial contributions from those who most would see as superstar achievers and true Performance Executioners. Some of these people include Bishop Desmond Tutu, Senator Elizabeth Dole, Pastor Joel Osteen, Warren Buffett, Suze Orman, Lee Iacocca, Tony Robbins, Coach Pat Summitt, Bill Cosby, Governors Arnold Schwarzenegger and Mitt Romney, Jim Stovall, Howard Dean, Tiger Woods, Linda Armstrong, James Carville, Mary Matalin, Donald Trump, President Bill Clinton, Steve Forbes, Deepak Chopra, Zig Ziglar, Coach John Wooden, Cherokee Nation Chief Chad Smith, Seminole Indian Tribe Chief Richard Bowers, Navajo Indian Nation Chief Joe Shirley, Russell Simmons, Sir Richard Branson, U.S. President Barack Obama and Andrea Jung. What became apparent from their contributions is that super-achieving individuals and super-achieving organizations look alike.

There are six fundamental truths or commonalities among every successful organization and individual you can study. While there may be more than six commonalities (traits, characteristics, patterns, behaviors, actions, etc.) which arise often among successful achievers, these are the only consistencies among them. So consider each as a benchmark, and as we work through each one, thoroughly chronicle how you presently perform and how each relates to you.

As performance achievers throughout the world reveal themselves daily, it becomes evident that one of the major impediments to our domestic success is our self-destructive behaviors or habits. I believe "adages" can provide us with powerful reference points for greater success and serve as beacons to warn against potential "suc" zones. Consider how often you have lived in these situations, and finish the adage if you can. (If you cannot, find a successful person to help you.)

1. We tend to be our own worst enemies, because many of us are creatures of _____!

2. Even though there are ways to be significantly more successful, many of us resist because you can't teach an old dog new _____!

3. People who could have had the capacity to be successful will not, because far too often we have the blind leading the _____!

.4. Even though all the resources and knowledge opportunities are available to become successful, most people are truly stubborn and resist like an old horse. You know this is true because you can lead a horse to water, but you can't _____!

5. A major obstacle to self-success is that many people tend to judge books by the _____, thus missing great opportunities for success and Performance Execution.

6. For most people, it is after the fact (and after our emotions calm), that we see solutions, answers, and resolution so easily. Could that be because hindsight is always twenty _____?

7. Of course, these adages all make sense to you because I am preaching to the _____!

So let's explore these six fundamental commonalities (adages) among every successful person, organization, and enterprise today to determine how they afford the unique ability to deliver Performance Execution!

The world is full of individuals willing to assign blame, affix responsibility for problems, and participate in bitching as a competitive sport. But few of these same individuals have a viable solution for anything!

Performance Execution starts and ends with setting yourself (and others) up for pure success. To do this, you must understand the four cornerstones of the "**Ownership Model®**." Ensuring success and the things which drive ownership comes down to the victories you have and can experience repeatedly. There are six fundamental ways for individuals and organizations to attain Performance Execution greatness.

First Truth – Victory analysis is driven by a tough-love understanding of your "**X-Factor®**." What this concept reveals for individuals on a generational platform, teams/departments, business organizations, or any enterprise, is significant to everything you will ever do or attempt to do from this point forward. This serves as the core driver to everything you should do and of what you must let go!

Grasp this concept and unleash the hidden potentials within you and those around you. Grasp this concept, and you can administer personal tough love and empower others to achieve levels of greatness that will mystify all who observe.

Second Truth – You must be willing to park your vanity and wimpy emotions on the sideline and fully understand and respect the magnitude of the X-Factor concept. From there, what is needed is an objective and thorough analysis of your competencies. This will enable you to hold yourself and others accountable for applying yourself to that at which you truly have the capacity to excel, and once and for all, drop that at which you are destined to always fail!

Only through the understanding and dogged utilization of "**The Player Capability Index®**" do you reveal where your X-Factor may be, and where it can be further grown and concentrated. This will radically change how individuals are hired, promoted, and tasked with further opportunities!

Here, you must get real with yourself and recognize what your X-Factor is and what the realities of possible future X-Factors are.

When you understand and apply this truth/model, then and only then can you really become objective in your analysis of others. Here is where you learn how to get beyond the outside vessel of a person and determine what assets really lie within them!

Third Truth – The ability to attain peak performance and fluidly execute decisions is reliant upon your ability to continuously make yourself relevant for the environment you are in and the market you serve. To do this, you must continuously apply the "**USFx2x4®**" model and recognize that all transactions of ownership revolve around this concept and the applicability of it to everything you do to differentiate yourself from others. There are four psychological drivers to our decision process, and you can always identify ways to ensure that you are relevant and explore ways to continuously reinvent yourself for Performance Execution.

This drives what an individual's and an organization's X-Factor should be!

With this enhanced understanding of how you can recognize your X-Factor and the multiple applications of that X-Factor, Performance Execution can accelerate to greater heights. With this model, organizations can get real about what their X-Factor is and is not!

Fourth Truth – Building alignment with others, or determining how best to integrate with other individuals and organizations can be driven through the understanding and sequential integration of five "**Mission Statements**". Understanding each mission statement, and how each mission statement chronologically influences the others, determines every choice you make. It also determines which you should not make, and how decisions are implemented among peak performers for more efficient change and stress management. This subsequently reveals itself very clearly in productivity and profitability charts!

Alignment of multiple X-Factors brings individual people and competing business units together in harmony.

Never before have the five independent links been connected. They can also now accelerate greatness and serve as guideposts to determine the source of cancers that can derail you and others from attaining true Performance Execution greatness.

Fifth Truth – A major differentiator between those who achieve greatness and those on the sidelines of life is the ability to make decisions and implement them. Here you will recognize that personal preferences, personality styles, and social upbringings have wired most people to be unable to make and facilitate decisions in a timely manner. Luckily, a four-step sequential "**STOP Decision Analysis Model®**" affords you a simplistic matrix to move forward and increase the output for which you strive!

Sixth Truth – Probably the most critical Performance Execution trait for sustained personal and professional success is the ability to realize that you are the sum whole of those people (not places) that occupy your mental real estate. Your Master Mind, Mental Board-of-Directors, or what I call your "**Mental Teeter-Totter®**" which directly influences your "**FIST Factor®**" is the understanding that these mental influencers drive your trajectory in life, and thus, destiny. (Within an organization, these are the factors that are engineered environmentally to impact culture in either a constructive or a destructive way!)

There are six fundamental commonalities of Performance Execution and super-achievers, so please stay with me to learn what they are.

You can look into the mirror of life and see the personal applications of these ideas, as well as reflect upon how you can engineer the environment to encourage others to attain peak Performance Execution as well. Here is where it begins and where it ends: taking ownership of our position and not obfuscating our responsibilities.

Again, newsflash, there is no SECRET!

Only ANSWERS!

You only arrive at the answers by asking tough, inwardly-directed QUESTIONS. From these questions the answers always reveal themselves. Then, and only then, can you unlock your SECRET to success!

Chapter Zero

Stand Up, Shut Up & Take Ownership, or Step Off the Planet:

Driving Yourself or Others to Take OWNERSHIP...
The Cancer Killing Individuals and Organizations Today!

Chapter Zero, ground zero, the foundation stage to pure performance success...Every person, parent, colleague, and employer struggles daily to understand why most people abdicate responsibility and only a few assume OWNERSHIP, whether it is ownership of a cause, project, activity, situation, job, etc.

So let's explore from where these six fundamental commonalities among every successful person, organization, and enterprise today and tomorrow come. It is these commonalities which afford individuals and organizations the unique ability to deliver Performance Execution!

Stand Up, Shut Up & Take Ownership, or Step Off the Planet

Performance Execution starts with setting yourself (and others) up for pure success. To do this, you must understand the four cornerstones of the Ownership Model®. Ensuring success and the drivers to ownership comes down to the victories you have and can experience repeatedly.

Take ownership, control your destiny!
Blame others, live in infamy!

Global war on talent is your new reality. Within a successful individual's and organization's operational DNA, consider:

Fifty-six percent of current employees actively report that they are "disengaged" in the workplace, and more than 15 percent report that they are "actively disengaged," according to a recent Gallup Organization study. WOW! More than 70 percent of employees are just taking up space. This was subsequently reinforced by an even more alarming survey done by the Conference Board, a private research group based in New York! (2010 data release).

If you wish to benchmark this data, put on a customer hat and go out and chronicle the level of customer care you experience today. Become your own undercover customer or boss to your own organization for a real performance execution reality check

A company's ability to gain a marketable and manageable advantage in today's business environment is critical to both its survival and its growth. This program focuses on how individuals within organizations manage resources and develop leadership skills to lead people on their teams and within their spheres of influence.

Creating a climate in which individuals assume ownership of their actions, tasks, and the reputation of an organization comes down to a simple sequence of interlinked actions. In working with profit and non-profit sector organizations over the past decade, a clear model has arisen that differentiates the winners from the losers – those that are successful versus those that "suc."

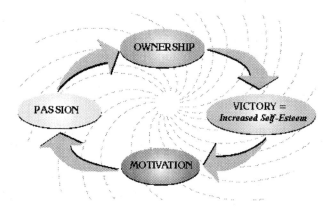

A.G. Lafley, CEO of Proctor & Gamble (P&G), has, in the first decade of this new century, made this exceedingly evident during his tenure by reshaping a world consumer products organization into an even greater brand. "The best way to drive success is to innovate…sustained organic growth!" as Lafley calls it. In creating this winning organization whereby everyone rises to the level of owning their sphere of influence, he says "individuals execute when individuals have a sense of fearlessness when it comes to failure!"

As the CEO, Lafley has assumed ownership and spun off $100-million-dollar business products and units that could not make their business model success ratios. Others in the business world would have been pleased with such profits based upon micro-vision and immediate gains. At P&G, however, ownership dictates that you maintain a macro perspective and big picture needs.

Winning organizations and individuals assume ownership and do not engage in the excuse game for not attaining performance expectations. How you go about assuming ownership (and creating a climate whereby others assume ownership of their jobs, responsibilities, themselves, and the overall organization) can be achieved by understanding how four factors are interlinked, and thus, where your first energies must be directed.

The burning question in the mind of most individuals is, "How do we go about getting others to assume a higher level of ownership?" With this question in mind, I began my homework assignment and learned the following:

1. When you know the depth of your skill abilities (formal and informal education, technical and non-technical training, certification and credentialed work, accolade experiences, etc.) and you draw upon and apply them appropriately, you experience success in accomplishment, or a self VICTORY. When you experience a VICTORY, your self-esteem goes up!

The same then holds true in your engagement of others.

2. When you are victorious, you become significantly more MOTIVATED about applying yourself, assuming more responsibility, and participating. At this point, the need to establish incentive and motivation programs becomes less necessary!

3. When you become MOTIVATED about seeing your victories and successes, you become significantly more PASSIONATE about life and the endeavors you pursue.

4. We take OWNERSHIP of those things and people about which we are passionate.

5. Getting people to take more ownership starts by setting them up for VICTORY!

How I realized this model was doing reverse analysis of some of the most successful businesses today, Many of whom are my own clients including:

Harley-Davidson, Army National Guard, Walmart, Boeing, Target, Anheuser-Busch, SeaWorld, and many more. I found that Performance Execution is about accomplishing meaningful outcomes.

To do this, the starting point is not "ownership" issues at all, but rather setting yourself up for victories and success.

Owners own ownership.
Losers lose, whine, and blame others!

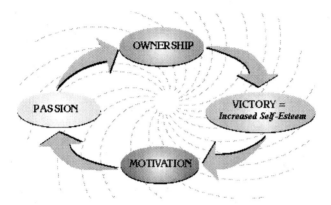

Look at the model again and realize that to make the model move forward, the starting point is VICTORY. This always puts performance in motion for execution.

People who assume OWNERSHIP seem to be among the most PASSIONATE for what they do. Those who have high passion for what they do are continuously MOTIVATED by what they do. This only happens when people are set up for VICTORIES by doing those things which they are best mentally and physically equipped to undertake. All of this feeds their self-esteem. When you operate from a level of high self-esteem, it is both exciting to see what you can accomplish and revealing to see what causes you to assume OWNERSHIP!

In his classic book "Good to Great," Jim Collins used the bus as a metaphor for leadership teams (businesses, departments, work units, etc.). He indicated that success, and thus, avoidance of "suc", are about getting the right people on your bus, the wrong people off your bus, and the remaining people on the bus in the right places. The bus metaphor could be expanded to be an entire group, or an individual's way of seeing themselves, and what they should, or should not do.

For you to attain greater and sustained levels of success, you first must shed some mental childhood DNA, as most people today play from a mental reference that almost assures that they "suc."

Want to know what I mean? Think about how many times you have heard or told someone:

1. Identify that at which you excel in life and always be looking for opportunities to apply yourself there. Heard that line before? If so, continue with that level of operation – this breeds success!

2. Identify that at which you excel and recognize that at which you are weak. Then when you find yourself having to do something that is not a strength, you can draw upon some of your strengths to complement your weaknesses and most likely prevail and be successful. Heard that line before? If so, continue with that level of operation – this breeds success!

3. Identify what your core or net weaknesses are and then apply yourself and work to overcome them. Heard that line before? If so, do not continue with that level of operation, or you will most assuredly "suc" forever!

When a person experiences a lack of VICTORIES, ask the powerful question, "What does this do to their MOTIVATION?" Once that is answered, then ask what that does to their PASSION. With that answer, it becomes very clear why people do not want to assume more OWNERSHIP of the situations, activities, projects, or jobs which continue to set them up to "suc"!

Either you are an active participant in the problem, or you are an active participant in the solution! Either way, you are taking an ownership stake and participating!

Need an example? There was a gentleman who lived in Chicago and played a little basketball. He became known by most measurements as someone who excelled at professional basketball, set all the records, and had the attention and respect of Madison Avenue and Main Street, USA. Then he tried his hand at professional baseball. It did not take him (nor anyone else) very long to realize that at basketball, he was an undisputed success, and at baseball, he "suc"-ed. According to the above logic, he followed one and two and abdicated number three. Who was this person? Michael Jordan.

Why do children and adults avoid taking ownership of what people expect of them? Why do you seem to shy away from excitedly taking control of something and executing a high level of performance success? The reason is due to three factors taken directly from the preceding diagram:

1. We tend to not volunteer or sign up for endeavors which do not play to our abilities. This drives us toward non-victories, which in turn, drives our self-esteem downward. Who wants to keep doing something that is embarrassing or makes them look stupid in the eyes of their peers?

2. With lackluster victories, we find that we spend a disproportionate amount of time trying to motivate ourselves or others in an attempt to do the things that do not inwardly and innately excite us anyway. Why? Because they do not play to our strengths in the first place (more on this in the next two chapters)!

3. Because we are not excited about what we are doing or those with whom we are associating, we have to fake the feeding of our passion. We engage in ceremonial activities, events, and celebrations to force-feed our appearance of being passionate. This, in turn, manifests as an individual's lack of stepping up to an opportunity and assuming ownership. Then we are left with abdication, excuses, procrastination, and people seemingly being oblivious to needs and situations.

Notice that most people live by warped logical mental blueprints or have mental DNA destined for the "suc" zone.

While working as Boeing's longest-invited leadership consultant/performance speaker (at the Boeing Leadership Center), and strategizing with their global Human Capital Development leaders (while simultaneously working with Anheuser-Busch's leadership development team) it became clear that in order to create ownership DNA within new professionals who were added to their teams, it was vital to ensure that people were positioned for victories, and that systems and environments were created to support this endeavor!

You can see this concept play out with positive (or unfortunately, far too often, with negative) results, as you look at major businesses. Systems have matured which allow individuals with success and victories to ascend upward into positions that they can truly screw up. This is not a commentary on them as people. I am sure that, in most cases, these are good people who mean well, but the reality is that they are placed into positions and expected to assume ownership, even though they lack the competency to execute their roles as true performers.

This is additionally adversely impacted by their vanity, which precludes them from asking for help.

Owners sign the front of a check. Losers own the experience of signing the back of checks, while blaming the name on the front for why they are poor!

This model holds true whether talking about the blue-collar aspects of the organization or the white-collar side of the organization. Whether engaging professionals within the Centurion or Baby-Boomer Generation (aka LinkedIn and Twitter), or the younger, entry-level side of Generation X, Generation Y (aka FaceBook), or the YouTube / Millennials / MTV / Nexter Generation (aka MySpace). (see Appendix One for Performance Execution application with differing generational segmentations)

There has to be a way to transition yourself and others away from "suc" and always towards success, wouldn't you think?

That would be a resounding YES, and this is how you do it! In order to create a universe in which you and others assume OWNERSHIP of your positions in life and become victors instead of victims, there are six specific ways every successful person and organization go about doing it!

Some organizations engineer a culture of one-team, one-organization, and thus, one-success. Southwest Airlines posted 90 consecutive quarters of profitability at a time when practically all other airlines sustained continued deficit operations, bankruptcy management, and a cutback mentality. How, you may ask, could Southwest Airlines do this? Simple. They instill into every employee and team member at every level that if the organization is not the choice of consumers, they do not make money. If they do not make money, no one wins in the end. While most major legacy airlines boast jet turnaround times of 45 to 60 minutes, with between eight and twelve ramp professionals, Southwest can turn a jet in 13 to 30 minutes, with three professionals.

Everyone at Southwest understands that when a jet is on the ground, the team loses money. As a result, everyone has a sense of "urgency" to assist in any way possible and ensure the jet is turned expeditiously. They are a team that assumes ownership in multiple ways to ensure Performance Execution!

There is never a lack of people who are envious of others' accomplishments, but I have never seen a line of people who are envious of the work it took to generate those accomplishments – have you?

Chapter One

Truth One:

The X-Factor® Is All That Counts in Life. Period.

Play to Your X-Factor and Always Be Successful!

PQ Reality Check: Successful organizations and people do what they are best at and let go of the rest. Remember, it is better to be thought a fool than to open your mouth and prove it.

Thus, it is better to be known as a successful organization or person for doing that at which you are truly gifted. Don't become known as the one who "sucs" because systems, processes, procedures, tenure, or vanity have caused you to enter into doing something that you have no business doing!

Let's explore the first truth of the six fundamental commonalities among every successful person, organization, and enterprise which affords them the unique ability to deliver Performance Execution!

This next PQ variable may radically change how you see yourself and others. It may give cause to radically reevaluate succession planning, promotion platforms, and the concept of tenure-driven paradigms for a more relevant, performance-driven paradigm. And most importantly, it will remove the traditional union mentality and enterprises that protect pathetic employees and behaviors at the cost of PQ team members and a PQ enterprise!

The X-Factor is All That Counts in Life. Period!

FIRST – Victory analysis is driven by a tough, self-love understanding of your X-Factor and what it reveals about individuals, teams/departments, business organizations, and any other enterprise. This serves as the core driver to everything you should do and of what you must let go in life – personally and professionally!

The "X" in X-Factor represents an endeavor, and is, in essence, anything that you would like to track. Let "X" represent the word success. Now, mentally frame the word by how you would define that word.

"Whether you believe you can or believe you cannot, you are absolutely correct!"
– Henry Ford

How would you define success? No matter what you say, you are correct. Some examples of how people define success are:

1. Happiness
2. Peace
3. Respect of others
4. Integrity
5. Material possessions
6. Career
7. Family
8. Community standing or involvement
9. Finances
10. Inspirational drivers
11. Social standing, involvement, or acceptance
12. Health
13. Education
14. Spirituality
15. Other

No matter how you define success within "The X-Factor," you are correct in your definition. Applying the concept so you can see how to set yourself and others up for Performance Execution success is what we want to work through in this chapter.

Performance Execution is about how you can avoid the "suc-factor" in life. At this point, you still do not understand the magnitude behind this concept or what the three little letters, "suc," really mean. So please work along with me as I explain.

Let's use "athletics" to represent the X-Factor. If we were to look at any high school campus on any given day of the school year, my first question would be:

1. Of one hundred percent of the kids on any high school campus on any given school day, what percentage of those students would be good enough to make it onto any varsity sporting team? What percentage number comes to your mind? There is no wrong answer, and there is no statistical data to confirm this model, so just use your gut and common sense to drive your

answers. What did you say? One, five, ten, maybe twenty percent would be good enough to make the varsity team?

2. Now, of one hundred percent of the estimated 1.1 million varsity high school athletes (NCAA/CBS Sports digest data 2008-2009) on high school campuses on any given school day, what percentage would be good enough to earn a scholarship to go onward and play at the collegiate level? What percentage comes to your mind? Again, there is no wrong answer, and there is no statistical data to confirm this model. Just use your gut and common sense to drive your answers. What did you say? Less than one, five, or maybe ten percent would be good enough to make the collegiate varsity team level?

3. Notice that if what we are tracking as the X-Factor endeavor is athletics, the more proficient we expect someone to be, the smaller that population pool becomes. Correct?

4. Finally, of one hundred percent of the estimated 28,800 collegiate varsity athletes, how many would be good enough to move onward and play that sport (their X-Factor) at the professional level? What percentage number comes to mind? Less than three, two, or one percent would be good enough to make the professional level, right?

5. The point is, as you look at yourself and that which you do, you are the "professional." Whatever the percentage you said for number four above is you. However, the bigger point is that not everyone can do what you do!

So what would lead you to believe that you can be a pro at everything? Better yet, why should the people we sometimes elevate with expectations of greatness be able to perform in every position or situation into which we place them as a professional? These are unrealistic expectations.

Make sure that you reflect upon the life-changing and life-impacting revelation of the X-Factor model. Using your math, here is what it looks like:

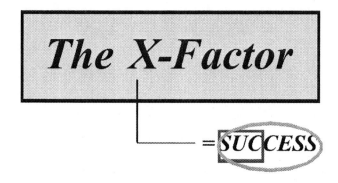

From the five previous questions, you and I can/could, at best, be a success (circled above) twenty percent of the time. The other eighty percent of the time we… notice what has a box around it in the X-Factor…

WOW!

Recognize that we have been saying "suc" and not "suck." Again, using the five previous questions as a reference to better understand the X-Factor concept, eighty percent of the time one would "suc". Now you can see the difference between setting yourself or someone else up for success versus "suc"!

The point is very clear. High-performance stars and those who understand Performance Execution limit their exposure to those things at which they know they "suc", and increase their exposure to opportunities to excel in areas in which they know they are "successful"!

Michael Jordan is a powerful example of the X-Factor in play. Need another example? Let's consider Louis Gerstner. He is the only person in the past few decades to have been the CEO of three different Fortune 500 firms, (American Express, RJR, and IBM) each of which was on the brink of bankruptcy when he arrived and all of which were highly profitable upon his departure!

Most likely, upon his arrival at American Express, it went something like this… He came in, sat down, and eyed his executive team. They eyed him back, and the expectation was that Mr. Gerstner had some magical X-Factor that would turn the firm around and aim it toward profitability once again. Instead, he opened a discussion with his executive team, having each person explain the road to success as they saw it. This conversation gave each team member the opportunity to share their X-Factor. When the conversation came full circle, he stood, announced that they all had the right answers, and his job was to support them during the execution of their game plans. As he left, they gave him a standing ovation. He learned at that moment that whenever you are in the "suc" zone, someone around you will be in the success zone. You merely need to let them shine, and lead everyone else to success.

In fact, there is an adage to this affect. "It is better to be thought a fool, than to open your mouth and remove all doubt." Gerstner recognized his X-Factor, and he drew upon the X-Factor of others to attain a new level of success.

The danger of this formula is that once applied, it will change the outcome of how you see yourself and how you view others. The tough love that is born from this concept may, more often than not, be applied because people really do like to "suc" and continue their "Oh, pity me," victim status. There are actually constituents that benefit from people remaining uniformed, uneducated, underemployed and underutilized!

Look deeply inside to the mirror of life, pronounce that at which you "suc", and stop doing it. Identify that at which you are destined to be a success, and live there!

It is critical to realize that Performance Execution comes from having as many people as possible positioned in their respective X-Factor zones and then getting out of their way. Recognize that when you are in your "suc" zone, there is a great likelihood that someone around you is in that same zone, although they could be in the success zone. It is important to recognize that although you may "suc" at something, someone else is "successful" at it. Have that person rise to the level of opportunity to assume ownership and lead others (and that can mean you) to Performance Execution greatness.

When you play from your X-Factor, it affects every decision you make, and thus, influences the trajectory of your life.

To observe an industry, a profession, and individuals that really grasp this concept (and truly live and die by continual, real-time assessment designed to ensure that they both live their X-Factor and welcome continuous feedback by any means possible), do not look at the mainstream business world or government agencies, because none of them grasp this concept. Instead, look at the world of professional athletics!

If you were a professional athlete, would you:

1. Have someone tape your performance for analysis immediately afterward, in hopes of attaining more performance "juice" and success?

2. Have someone tape your practices for review at regular intervals, in hopes of attaining more performance "juice" and success?

3. Review the tape of your competitor's performance for analysis, in hopes of attaining more performance "juice" and success?

4. Review the tape(s) of the best athletes in your industry to benchmark your performance in hopes of attaining more performance "juice" and success?

I imagine the answer to each of these four questions would be a resounding YES!

Therein lies the reason why an athlete is either in their X-Factor zone and successful, or they fade from the spotlight very quickly. Only the best of the best survive. They do so by first playing to their X-Factor, second, continuously seeking out performance feedback, and third, working to refine and improve their skill set.

Therein, also, lies a major factor explaining why most people outside of professional athletics "suc". Organizations' performance review systems are inadequate, mathematically-driven to support tenure-driven dynamics and not Performance Execution dynamics, and are facilitated far too infrequently to have relevant applications. To make X-Factor identification, development, and attainment even more challenging, most people become defensive when receiving performance feedback instead of accepting it for what it is, and acting upon it openly.

Take a tough look at yourself, reflect upon the personal applications, and apply this same approach to the organizations in which you participate. With this concept and model in mind, you now need an objective, quantitative tool to either determine what your true X-Factor is, or to afford you the framework to grow yourself and/or others to possess the needed X-Factors!

Those who recognize what their X-Factors are, and can operate at that level, find that they make significant, meaningful contributions to themselves, others, the organizations they serve, and their communities as a larger whole. They truly are "*VIPs*"! (Very Important People/Players/Performers)

Unfortunately, we have created a world wherein people are allowed to play from their true "suc-factors," and we still treat them as if they are VIPs, when in reality, they are "*VUPs*" (Very Unimportant/Unimpressive People/Players) who have devolved to a pathetic level of contribution and are falsely propped up and compensated as if they were VIPs!

Want another vivid example of how people who play to their "suc-factor" can create less-than-successful outcomes?

In 2008, the United States Congress was faced with a significant financial challenge stemming from the uncontrolled actions of FreddieMac and FannieMae, along with complacent Wall Street giants' actions, and spurred on by the partisan media and political leaders that had been allowed to play off of their "suc-factor" for an extended period of time. So what did Congress and the President do? They hammered out a band-aid solution that none of the players intellectually grasped. In fact, when a glossary of terms had to be hastily prepared so the Speaker of the House, the President, and key Democratic and Republican leaders could understand the subject matter, it should have given one of them a clue about the X-Factor concept and how to act next, however, it did not.

It is not realistic for anyone to always be in the "success factor zone," but it is critical to recognize when you are in the "suc-factor zone" and not prove it!

In these times, it is imperative for Performance Execution stars to downplay emotions and finger-pointing, and hold individuals accountable for their actions. For example, according to a BBC World News documentary that aired in October 2008, under repeated briefings and congressional hearings from 2003 through 2005 by then U.S. Secretary of Treasury, John Snow, and Federal Reserve Board Director, Alan Greenspan, the Bush Administration made repeated calls for more regulation, anticipating the impending financial implosion on Capitol Hill. Yet congressional leaders Barney Frank (D-MA), Charles Schumer (D-NY), Harry Reid (D-NV), and Nancy Pelosi (D-CA), during this same time are on the record, denouncing each of the White House warnings, repeatedly saying FreddieMac and FannieMae were doing fine, and regulations would only cause harm to a great and growing segment of the economy. (As you read this, do not allow yourself to excuse away this sentence by assuming I am simply a Republican, as you would be wrong on both accounts!)

If these players in Washington had understood the X-Factor concept and the concepts of Chapters Two and Five in this book, what they should have immediately done is:

1. Called, subpoenaed, demanded, invited to Washington D.C., or had ushered in by the United States Marshall Service if necessary, the best financial minds in America to consult on this issue; seeing as the elected political representatives were obviously out of their intellectual X-Factor depths. Imagine the conversation and synergy of ideas if a cross-section of American Performance Execution minds were consulted, such as: Warren Buffett, Bill Gates, Steve Forbes, Suze Orman, Mitt Romney, Donald Trump, George Kaiser, Oprah Winfrey, Alan Greenspan, and any other legitimate, stand-out financial/entrepreneurial leaders.

2. Called, subpoenaed, demanded, invited to Washington D.C., or had ushered in by the United States Marshall Service, if necessary, the best financial, tax, and legal minds in America from all appropriate trade associations which comprise the spectrum of industries involved in the crises. Their consultation on this issue would have been beneficial, since the politicians were out of their intellectual X-Factor depths.

3. Run a quick scan of Congress (based upon true credentials) for any members who actually had a resume of clues to assist the appointed committee and/or senior congressional leadership when it became even more apparent that they were out of their X-Factor depths.

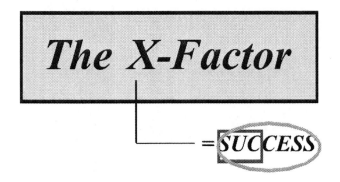

4. Put in place major control mechanisms (from the onset) for government ownership of the companies which were being bailed out, to help ensure later financial gain for the people as a whole.

Instead, what happened was that individuals recognized that, as a whole, they were out of their X-Factors and were more interested in making sure they would get re-elected. So they abdicated being Americans and opted for being politicians. Eighty-plus percent of the "nay" votes by members of Congress were cast because those politicians were up for re-election. The American financial market lost more than $1.1 trillion dollars, and the stock market plunged more than it had in twenty years – WOW!

So where did this idea originate? The last time it was done was during World War II, when the heads of every major aviation organization (Mr. Boeing, Mr. Hughes, Mr. Douglas, Mr. McDonnell, etc.) were summoned to Washington, D.C. to address how to step up the war effort, and transport the soldiers and equipment that needed to be air-lifted immediately from America to Europe.

Additional proof that we, as Americans, truly do value losers (and elect political leaders that "suc") is the latest bailout plan. It actually had add-on pork barrel entitlements for projects that had nothing to do with the crises at hand – WOW we are stupid!

Because people tend to be creatures of habit and judge books by their covers, people also tend to let their vanity and egos override their common sense and logic. This propels many into playing to their "suc-factor" and not their "success factor!"

So how do you ensure that you and those you can influence will be Performance Execution stars, VIPs, (more on this term in the next chapter) and meaningful contributors to the planet? This next model is critical for objective analysis of ourselves, (tough self-love time is coming up in the next chapter) and those with which we come into contact – whether we plan to coach, promote, or hire them.

I do not expect elected political leaders, business leaders, or any of us as individuals to be in the "success factor" zone on every topic, but we most certainly need to recognize when we are in the "suc-factor" zone, so we don't prove it!

When people let their vanity cloud their actions and play from their "suc-factor," the result is the blind leading the blind!

If people grasp this model and the next chapter's model, you've successfully taught an old dog a new trick, thus turning them into creatures of success habits!

If you grasp it and utilize it, your decision flow will change in about twenty minutes, for life! You will see yourself and others differently. You will start to recognize why past Performance Execution attempts may have failed, and what you can start to do to attain higher levels of Performance Execution success in life – in twenty minutes!

Chapter Two

Truth Two:

The Player Capability Index® Calls Your Bluff for Ultimate Talent Management Objectivity:

The Player Capability Index® Reveals Your X-Factor & Catapults Individuals Forward – It's Your IQ Plus EQ That Equals Your Ultimate PQ!

Let's explore the second truth of the six fundamental commonalities among every successful person, organization and enterprise which affords them the unique ability to deliver Performance Execution!

Second – Objective talent management and thorough analysis of your competencies through the understanding and dogged utilization of **The Player Capability Index**® reveals what your X-Factor may be, where it can be further grown and honed, and most importantly, what it is not.

This next commonality will radically change your internal and external conversations. It will radically change how you see yourself and others. It will radically change how organizational systems are run and business individuals are hired, promoted, and tasked with further opportunities. This next fundamental commonality is an objective diagnostic tool that will impact your PQ!

The Player Capability Index Calls Your Bluff

Imagine you are a time machine. Your mind either focuses forward through the windshield of life (Performance Execution / performance success and future tense) or it keeps flashing into the rearview mirror of life, so it can excuse away everything you never attained and why you are not progressing, thus living in the past!

The corporate think-tank known as the Conference Board, recently conducted a survey of hundreds of top businesses and thousands of corporate professionals

(2008/2009 survey data) and found that:

1. Fifty-six percent of survey respondents indicated that they are "disengaged" in the workplace.

2. Seventeen percent of survey respondents indicated that they are "actively disengaged" in the workplace.

Thus, seventy-three percent of workers are not in their X-Factor and are looking for ways to provide minimal effort for maximum payment. Even worse, many times, these people are not set up for success by those who have influence and are charged with the development of employees as Human Capital / organizational assets.

Imagine the level of effectiveness and Performance Execution you could experience if these players with these attitudes had their futures freed up, so that someone with integrity, drive, and self-worth could have their job opportunities.

We get what we tolerate, and we get what we measure and for what we hold others accountable. The squeaky wheel gets the grease.

Recently, while working with the American Institute of Certified Public Accountants (AICPA) and the CEOs of the largest 100 CPA firms in America, a real-time electronic survey was facilitated with these CEOs on the issues of Human Capital performance and the competency capital, within their respective organizations. Three major points became very evident:

1. Most (not all) have a Human Capital strategic plan for the development of their employees, the cultivation of future talent, and the succession plan thereof...Lesson Learned – Do You?

2. The majority never reference the most recent twelve-month cycle as a tool to gauge their policies, guide their actions, or drive their internal development procedures...Lesson Learned – Do You?

3. When a partner or key Human Capital player leaves their team, the majority begin the succession development and transition of responsibilities as a real-time endeavor in the concluding six to twelve months...Lesson Learned – What Do You Do?

Ask yourself if any of these comments may be reflective of you or someone within your organization as a reality in growing individuals and making them more valuable within your community. The same is important for organizational leadership development needs and forecasts.

As a performance coach to coaches, educators, and professionals alike, what alarms me the most is that people and organizations no longer see individual Human Capital development as a paramount need. People talk about it, but their budgets, commitments, and actions far too often yell the opposite.

To compound this variable, the Fortune 500 firm mentioned earlier, which had the worst product launch in their 100-plus year history, elevated the executive-in-charge afterwards and made that person responsible for the entire organizational learning and development enterprise. Instead of addressing personnel issues on the basis of true Performance Execution, many still feel obligated to operate from a tenure-based paradigm: "You have been here the longest. Let's promote you. It's your turn." Within just two short years, practically everyone that had been a part of that learning enterprise for the previous decade had bailed. It's kind of like saying to the executive, "Now that you have quantifiably proven that you "suc," and because we do not have the guts to terminate you, and are litigiously paranoid of a resulting discrimination suit, we are going to move you to train and develop the rest of us." To make this case study even more humorous, his tenure in the learning enterprise was less than a year before he was moved again to a different position within the company, thus creating a damaging legacy for a second business unit!

Many times people wonder why those around them - leaders, colleagues, politicians, friends, or even family members - who should excel, instead flounder. Often, we forget to truly ask, "What is this person's X-Factor? Do they even have an X-Factor?"

The reason we "suc" and others "suc" more is frequently the fact that we respond more to our emotions and what is popular than to what is sound, logical, and right to guide our actions, decisions, and encouragement of others.

If you do not stay focused, you, too could wake up one day and find yourself or your business imploding all around you...

But maybe it will not be a real surprise if you then look in the rearview mirror of life and recognize all of the warning signs that had been there all along.

Organizations often equate pay raises with promotions, and not actual contribution competency – Performance Execution quality and quantity.

So how do you ensure that you invest more time on the windshield (the future) and not the rearview mirror (the past)? How do you ensure your personal Human Capital index is always moving upward, onward and forward? The same way as a performance leader (employer, entrepreneur, boss, mentor, or even parent): you use objective tools to hold youself and others accountable.

Deploy the **Player Capability Index Model**° on yourself to ensure you know what your real Human Capital X-Factor is. Then apply it to others, so you can attain greater Performance Execution outcomes from them as well. From the following formula, we find that it is really a combination of your IQ and your EQ that drives your Performance Execution Quotient or your PQ!

Consider this diagnostic formula, whether computerized, reduced to an excel spreadsheet, built into online or hard copy employment applications, or used as a self-assessment. Ask yourself if you know the totality of response / answers to each formula "letter" as it pertains to you:

$$C = (T2 + A + P + E + C)E2 \times R = R$$

1. **R** = (starting on the far right side of the formula) Results or desires you need to generate or desire to generate. To get the R, you must know who you are, or objectively who the other person is.

2. **C** = Capability. Your C is derived from a combination of...

3. **T** = Training (which includes all education: formal and informal, technical and non-technical, certification and non-certification, etc.). Here, training represents your complete set of knowledge from your birth to the present tense. If you lack the T (training) necessary to have the C (capability), then a second T would stand for further, or future T development and acquisition you need.
   We'll indicate these two levels of your training as T2.

4. **A** = Attitude. Your desire, willingness, self-initiative, and self-confidence. Attitude is illustrated by how you act, talk, dress, and engage others. It is your attitude that drives your PQ, as drawn from the depth of your IQ and EQ.

5. **P** = Performance. This reinforces whether you know how to do something or not and shapes your overall capability levels. True X-Factor professionals seek continued 24/7 constructive feedback to always improve their performance abilities and standards of Performance Execution excellence, as well as benchmarking their efforts from those of other industry leaders for increased performance.

6. **E** = Experiences; which either enhance or hinder your capabilities. Run a mental inventory on yourself. Think of all of the people, places, and things that you have come into contact with, (from birth to today) which have (consciously or subconsciously) influenced who you presently are. This will give you critical insight into how you may or may not perform. Constructive, positive, nurturing experiences shape your performance in one direction and determine the outlook they possess. Conversely, the trauma and harm you have endured also come into play. These same types of forces can be deployed in your future to either further reinforce how you have been influenced or change how you may be influenced.

7. **C** = Culture you have experienced within your life up to the present time. The cultures of your personal and professional life combine to influence your capability, as well.

Once culture can be defined at a macro level, greater understanding can be gained by digging into any individual cultural variable at the micro level of your: ethnicity; gender; generational segmentation; geographical regionalization (continent, nation, state, county, city, rural, urban, etc.); organization (company, business, industry, division, team, work unit, etc.); socio-economic factors; family; ancestry; etc.

All of this combines to determine your net Human Capital DNA, but it is influenced on a regular basis by your:

8. **E** = Expectations. This formula is influenced by the power of the E2 on the outside of the equation or formula. There are two applications of expectation. It is **your** expectation(s) of yourself which drives your final performance output, which combines with the expectation(s) of the "other party" upon you to cause you to pull upon your $T+A+P+E+C$ to attain true peak Performance Execution effectiveness (or not).

You may possess a tremendous depth of deposits within each of these letters (T+A+P+E+C), but if you have a low set of expectations for yourself in any given situation, at best, you will bring your "B Game" to the office. So expectation really does become the driver to the capability level of an individual!

9. **R** = Relationships. This entire formula is influenced and can be enhanced or diminished based upon the relationships a person has and has had which influence the development of each DNA variable within the formula. The people that you know and those who know you can enhance or diminish your Player Capability Index. Leveraged effectively, your Relationships can allow you to showcase your inner power. Ineffectively utilized, your relationships can cause your best efforts to implode!

Imagine the influence this "R" (Relationship) has if you had a colleague or employee who was influenced from childhood by those who modeled deception, deceit, and arrogance. It would not be a surprise to have that person or employee take advantage of you and maintain a demeanor of ambivalence. Or imagine a person kicked out of college or someone who surrounds themselves with people who have sold their honor for material possessions. It would not be a stretch for that person to hijack your credentials and possessions as theirs to further their career or ambitions. Conversely, a person of honor and strong DNA variables can lead you and others to greatness.

With the insight gained from this formula you should be able, with a great level of accuracy, to forecast the performance of others in good times and crises situations. Likewise, look into a mirror and do some self reflection.

So how do you apply this to your life? Let's say you have been asked to do something, which becomes letter "R" (Results) in the formula. In order to determine whether the task is within your X-Factor domain, apply the other letters within the parentheses of the formula to yourself and determine the depth of each letter as it relates to you. The QUESTIONS that this model raises (re-read the Preface to put the QUESTIONS-ANSWERS-SECRET formula into context) will reveal the ANSWERS to your X-Factor – and the same can be applied to others.

People who run their lives without the use of this model are like ships with no navigational systems. Any port is welcome, even though it may be the wrong destination!

WOW! Imagine if we actually applied this diagnostic instrument to our social networks, those organizations which hire us as clients/employees/vendors/etc., to determine which individuals are targeted for promotions and which executive ascends upward...who is allowed onto a Board of Directors, and who we elect to public office!

Did you really read this formula and understand it?
This model is the enemy of partisan politicians, partisan journalists, partisan business leaders, and simple-minded partisan individuals in general. It takes the emotion directly out of a conversation and makes Performance Execution direction very clear!

A better understanding of the actual responses to each qualifying letter in the above model drives you to better understand your PQ and the PQ level of others. It is the combination of the IQ and EQ factors from above which help you arrive at your PQ!

Within organizations, associations, government, and your own personal interactions, have you ever known someone who possessed a tremendous depth of T, yet a world-class, crappy A? If so, they do not P very well, do they? Conversely you probably know people who may not have tremendous depth of T, but who do possess a great A, and they at least try to P all the time!

In nearly all vocations, the T can be provided, but the A is more difficult to cultivate. Now, use this as an overlay to organizations like Southwest Airlines and Harley-Davidson. You begin to see how they reinvented an industry and why they are market leaders, as the A is the central factor used in determining who is hired and promoted.

To attain higher levels of Performance Execution from yourself or others, consider how society and business models have, for decades, conditioned us to operate in a manner opposite to what this model directs.

Example: Consider that a typical job application and interview conversation centers around many topics and educational background information. It is in this area of "education" that we tend to overvalue formal education and devalue informal education. Yet, it is the informal adult education that is sought, and which is a multi-billion dollar industry. It is the endless array of seminars, workshops, rallies, symposiums, self-studies, home-studies, webinars, teleseminars, DVD courses, podcasts, satellite / internet / television educational and informational programs, electronic self-help books, distance learning offerings, live on-screen pop-up videos, etc. that people seek out for immediately-applicable needs in their careers. We drill and spend significant time to find out the highest level of education you possess, and from which disciplines and institutions. However, we spend very little – and, in far too many instances, no – time vetting our colleagues and prospective new hires to learn what T / Training they can bring to our disposal for immediate gains!

Want more evidence as to how powerful this model can be?

This will surely challenge some readers' emotions, but the utilization of this model will also help you keep yourself and others in logic check. Imagine you were to take the credentials of all the candidates in the 2008 United States Presidential race, as of January 2007, and diagnostically evaluate the resumes without seeing the individuals' names. What you would arrive at is the clear logic-based realization that BOTH the DNC and RNC/GOP nominated their least competent, qualified, credentialed, vetted candidates – WOW!

Both parties' partisan behaviors failed their fellow Americans.

While both men are great Americans, that is not what we are evaluating here. Neither of these men had ever signed a check in their professional lives (they had cashed checks, but never signed one). Neither individual ever worked in the commercial marketplace that comprises our free enterprise capitalist system to generate cash flow (one of the three primary reasons the United States of America was founded by our forefathers!). Neither had ever run any organization (either as a CEO of a business or Governor [CEO] of a State) prior to their campaign. They both had been members of teams and committees (which typically impede Performance Execution) on a regular basis by serving merely as members of congressional committees for the majority of their professional tenures.

If the model were used, both parties would have had exceedingly qualified candidates to present to Americans. But we have devolved into a popularity-driven media contest for the presidency – not a competency-based endeavor.

Interestingly, we have 54 candidates for Miss America, yet only two for the presidency?

If you want to search Performance Execution at the highest level and observe even more clearly what happens when you let emotion and popularity, instead of competency, lead your actions, continue to run the **Player Capability Index®** model on the two presidential candidates or anyone else. Would you hire yourself for what you currently do?

Performance Execution stars always surround themselves with UP!

If you were to apply this new matrix, you would always hire up, promote up, and associate up. Far too often, the reality is that individuals charged with making things better are easily intimidated by subscribers to Performance Execution. Therefore, more often than not, we see that they surround themselves with people who are always inferior to them, so they can always bee seen as superior to everyone else – when you hire and promote down, you dumb down!

> *"As" hire "As," and "Bs" hire "Cs" …*
> *Inventory with whom you surround yourself,*
> *and you will have a revealing past-to-present tense answer…*
> *Now you have another clue for how to succeed!*

Imagine if the media had the intellectual capacity to understand this model and then professionally, respectfully, and aggressively used this in vetting political candidates at any level, anywhere in the world. The asinine questions, interviews, debates, and sound-bite-driven world in which we live would appear radically different. Instead, we have driven away Performance Execution stars from many walks of life, where they are desperately needed, due to "gotcha" journalism and the never-ending hunger for what is in someone's closet instead of what is within their **Player Capability Index®**!

I am reminded of another colossal blunder resulting from executives failing to utilize a model like this, people losing their jobs, and millions of dollars being thrown away in bad or poorly-executed business decisions.

In the autumn of 2007 through the autumn of 2008, the airline Alitalia, partially owned by the Italian government, experienced an implosion. The employees protested and marched down the runways of the Athens, Greece airport. It had many of the same contradictions we have discussed thus far in this book and more – many similar to an American blunder from Houston-based ExpressJet.

ExpressJet, based in Houston, Texas, (which was previously the commuter feeder airline to Continental Airlines) launched their own service to a new target market. While they had a superior product to offer and great employees on the frontline, it did not help outweigh a corporate leadership team that was clueless.

Each market they targeted made sense, and the flight crews delivered a stellar product experience for passengers, but the marketing campaign was a classic example of good people placed into positions beyond their intellectual capacity, making one textbook blunder after another. It is what I call the ABCs to business marketing blunders – attracting business via normal Acceptable Business Channels:

1. Major ads announcing their service were placed in local lifestyle magazines, daily newspapers, and billboards on the side of the highway.

2. The problem which would have easily been revealed if ExpressJet had applied the **Player Capability Index**® to the people making decisions is that they had the proverbial "blind leading the blind."

3. In one market they entered, research widely available to anyone on the ground in that local market indicated that the lifestyle magazines carrying their ads had a target demographic of forty-plus-year-old women, most unemployed, and not the high-purchase demographics of business travel tickets. The local newspaper's business section consisted of literally one to no more than five pages daily – with most of its content in wire download format. Clearly, the local press was neither business-savvy, nor business-friendly.

4. The billboard ads were in low traffic areas and posted in such a way that drivers could not read and understand the service offer.

5. When the new airline was presented with a comprehensive list of area business travelers, along with suggestions as to how to connect with actual travelers in the airport and places to place high impact ads and messages within the community, both the ExpressJet management team responsible for getting "butts in seats," and their New York City ad agency were highly offended. If one applied the **USFx2x4**® Model presented in the following chapter of this book, an endless list of high-impact customer contact ideas could have been created, and thus, subsequently applied to increase the odds of a successful and profitable market entry.

USFx2x4® examples of high-impact, low-financial-investment strategic ideas that were given to ExpressJet upon their entry into the market, yet never implemented (or implemented in a misguided manner) provided further textbook embarrassment. Some of the ideas suggested (which would have a consultation market value exceeding $250,000) included:

a. Place ads with an incentive to buy one ticket and get a same flight companion seat for less, or FREE – **never acted upon.**

b. Acquire a direct mail list of known business travelers from competitor airlines and make sure they knew of the new airline's options – **never acted upon.**

c. Acquire a list of local area business professionals from the Chamber of Commerce and begin a regular, sequential e-mail marketing campaign – **never acted upon.**

d. Provide all existing passengers with a coupon booklet, and instant frequent flyer membership, making it less attractive for them to remain a passenger with existing airline providers than to switch to the new airline's services – **never acted upon.**

e. Design a special marketing message to business owners, HR managers, travel department managers, and area travel agents, informing them about the new service, how it can save the user time and money, and how it can be a strategic business option for them to utilize – **never acted upon.**

f. Place strategic travel billboards inside airport terminals (where passengers are waiting for their flights) promoting their services and destinations. This would have been especially important in delayed and cancelled flight situations, informing potential passengers of ExpressJet's possibly unknown services as a solution to their travel needs which were currently being ignored by their competitor airlines – **never acted upon.**

i. They did (at the end of their lifecycle) post billboards inside terminals at baggage claim that promoted ExpressJet.

Unfortunately, the majority of business travelers do not check luggage, and therefore, would never see the misplaced signage!

g. Identify the high-impact travelers' trade associations in local markets which could provide both customers and advocates – **never acted upon.**

h. Create an entire viral marketing campaign that included pop-up marketing, banner ads, affiliate marketing lead generation, YouTube-style word-of-mouth and push-pull marketing, live video Internet messaging campaigns, text message campaigns, etc. – **never acted upon.**

6. From its inception, the average flight load of the airline never exceeded 50 percent.

The punch line to this example is that the airline industry's average lifecycle of new market entry to exit was less than twelve months in 2007 through 2009 – WOW!

Juxtapose this with Southwest Airlines' commanding profitability during each of these same quarters with expansion markets and new jets added to their fleet.

Performance Execution is about individuals taking responsibility and holding all those that would abdicate this responsibility in contempt!

By understanding the **Player Capability Index®** formula, you can now objectively recognize where you or others may fail due to expectations to perform from your actual "suc-factor" basis. Performance Execution comes only from playing to and from your X-Factor dominance.

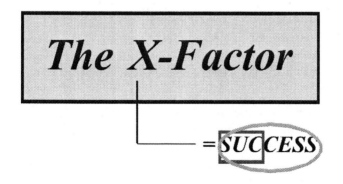

Again, return to the previous chapter's reference to the financial crises in America and how Congress responded. I cannot expect my elected leaders to be in the success factor zone on every topic, but I surely do not want to find them proving their "suc-factor." Imagine what level of response would have been administered if Congress had rallied together the best-of-the-best minds in the days immediately following the economic implosion.

Study any great athlete, performer, entrepreneur, or business leader, and you will recognize that this is one of their simple operational DNA mantras.

Tiger Woods at the height of his PGA career in the early 2000s, fired his coach, knowing that he was not as strong at the fundamentals as he needed to be. He returned to an earlier coach, and with this major change, went on to attain even greater accomplishments.

Here are several additional X-Factor, self-propelling, forward-momentum action plans to ensure performance excellence from you and those around you:

1. Brutally look out the window before you (your present tense reality and the future you wish to move into) and ask yourself if you possess, or have accessible to you through your sphere of influence, the Human Capital DNA necessary to attain true success. If the answer is no, do not accept the position before you; get people with the real Human Capital DNA to lead others forward at that moment in time (this is what Jim Collins, in his classic book GOOD TO GREAT, calls the Bus)!

   Stop letting yourself, your family members, colleagues, employees, and associates in an organization you are part of, position themselves for failure, or at best, mediocrity.

2. Make sure the members of your executive leadership team, or any team for that matter, are not all clones of one another. This breeds "group think." Diversity in gender, ethnicity, generation, competencies, and experience is critical! (refer to number 3 below for more)

Look at your organization and realize you can begin to forecast future decisions based upon your **Player Capability Index®** findings. Better yet, do not affiliate yourself with groups whose overall equation is so out of balance that they are destined for failure.

This is the very reason why the airline industry from 2000 through 2010 has been in such turmoil: an exceedingly unbalanced X-Factor.

3. Recognize that it is your IQ and EQ which form the great reserve of Human Capital abilities. Do you invest equally in each? Now, the turbo enhancer to all of this is actually your PQ, or Performance Execution Quotient!

4. Engage in 360-degree Human Capital learning from a mentor. Begin actively investing in others' Human Capital DNA by mentoring them, and build mentoring systems around you for the free fluid movement of Human Capital DNA!

5. Build a real-time Human Capital inventory of everyone around you that can be instantly accessed and easily administered for net needs, and appropriate assignment tasking. Imagine as a parent, teacher, mentor, manager, or leader, if you not only knew the depth of every person you engaged, but also had a systematic way to know these answers in real-time. Imagine being able to type into a system the requirements for something you needed done, and upon hitting enter, a list of only real-time, legitimate, candidates' names would be presented back to you.

The implications here on training, learning and development, tasking and delegating, and succession planning are enormous!

6. Create a Human Capital development plan tied into personal needs and windshield necessities for you and everyone you influence. Then demand nothing less than total adherence, commitment, and accomplishment to it!

7. What is an instant Human Capital endeavor you can commit to, to ensure that when you finish reading this book, you are forward windshield focused and do not digress into rearview mirror activities, negative self talk, or whining sessions with others?

8. Given that professional athletes are more serious about performance improvement and performance standards than those in most other industries, vocations, consider operating like an athlete. There are a few questions you will need to explore. What is the likelihood that a professional athlete would have their game performances chronicled / taped / recorded for immediate feedback by their trainer or coach? What is the likelihood

that they may have the same done for the practices? And what about their desire to review the performances of their major competitor? Of course, I am sure you said "yes" or "high" to each question. Start asking for real-time data collection and coaching to really improve your game-time life performance!

9.   Review the performance review instrument your team or firm uses and ask yourself if it really tracks the areas of your performance necessary for performance improvement feedback. If not, add them. Better yet, how often is it administered? If it is not administered on a monthly basis, at minimum, then why not inquire as to how your colleagues, boss, or even external key clients / customers can start to provide you with this valuable information on a more regular basis?

For a copy of a compiled super Performance Appraisal Instrument crafted from among 32 of America's top Fortune firms, send an e-mail to *Info@JeffreyMagee.com* and ask for it by name. A PDF copy will be sent free of charge. What is most striking about its high level of impact is that it is not a numerically driven assessment instrument and only allows for three performance -level scoring options from any measured category!

Imagine that you are now the time machine referenced at the beginning of this chapter. You choose whether your mind focuses forward through the windshield of life (performance success) or keeps flashing back into the rearview mirror of life (so it can excuse away everything you never attained and make excuses for not progressing forward)!

See yourself in your future… Now go live your future with a clear and objective tough-love understanding of where you must apply your energies!

Those who recognize the objective power of the Player Capability Index® model and the ramifications of elevating themselves and others around them, will find that they make continuous, significant, and meaningful contributions to others, the organizations they serve, and the community as a larger whole around them. These truly are the VIPs! It is these VIPs who enlarge the contributions to the planet and elevate Performance Execution to both an art form, and science. They have a hunger to always better what they do, and those with whom they associate.

Unfortunately, we have created systems, procedures, programs, policies, expectations, and paradigms in this world whereby people are not conditioned, expected, or even demanded to better themselves. They are allowed to play from their true "suc-factors," and we treat them as if they are VIPs as well, even though, in reality, they are VUPs who have broken down their expectations (and those of others) to a pathetic level of contribution and are falsely propped up and compensated as if they are VIPs!

Sad to say, it is a shocking commentary on individuals, organizations, and society that we many times accept, condone, and promote individuals without the Player Capability Index® firepower we need to attain success; then we complain when we do not get meaningful results. Or worse yet, we participate in the compensation, tolerance, promotion, elevation, and election of VUPs, and then, when they do not perform like VIPs, we become alarmed and pretend to be shocked.

I once had a performance-coaching client (a United States Congressman) with whom I terminated my relationship when it became clear that he preferred being a VUP at a time when his constituents desperately needed him to be a VIP. Case in point:

1. His own father stated, on the record, after the Congressman's election, that they were excited that he now had a job – WOW!

2. His resume indicated that his past jobs, in totality, did not warrant the electorate ever elevating him to Congress – says a lot about good marketing!

3. He received a pay raise when he became a Congressman that was over and above what he was earning as a private citizen. This should have been a major clue that the constituents were electing someone whose primary goal was going to be keeping that job, and not actually doing it!

4. While sitting in his office one afternoon, the conversation evolved into an awkward social situation that convinced me it was better for me to leave, and not consume any more of his time. Then, he continued, and ultimately asked me to slip out a back door with him, so he could avoid a previously scheduled meeting with local legal professionals and judges of the NAACP who were waiting for him.

5. It became apparent that he had gender employment issues after he terminated the women who had served him loyally during his election campaign. Later, he terminated a career civil service employee due to her physical disabilities. In order to keep this action out of reach of the media and his constituents leading up to his re-election bid, he settled the case out-of-court, and placed a gag order on it.

6. Finally, when we were flying together on a business trip, he remarked, "I can't wait until I have served enough terms to have my retirement package set, and to be able to then get me a PAC position like (insert name of a fellow Congressman we both knew, who is presently doing this) making millions of dollars a year!"

The VUPs who have not pushed themselves for continuous development of the individual components of the formula are really Very Unimpressive People / Players / Performers, and shame on them for taking up space on the planet!

As you reflect upon yourself, and observe out of the windshield of performance life around you, do you see players and organizations thriving and embracing objective diagnostic evaluation of individual capability levels, or do you see complacency as the norm?

This is exactly what Louis Gerstner learned as a major business leadership life lesson in attaining higher levels of Performance Execution. This name should be on every Performance Execution star's short list of mental mentors, as he is the only person to have served as the CEO of three Fortune 100 firms (American Express, RJR, and IBM), each of which was on the brink of bankruptcy when he arrived and were solidly sound and profitable upon his departure!

Lessons learned which incorporate understanding the X-Factor and the Player Capability Index® came from his arrival at American Express. Instead of telling the team there what must be done, he quickly grasped that, in large part, he was in his "suc-factor" and there was great likelihood that many of the individuals on his leadership team, if given the opportunity to shine, would demonstrate what their "success factors" were. So what he did was initiate a dialogue on what the team thought should be done to turn the organization around. After a series of conversations, he stood and simply said, "Let's do it."

There is an adage that embodies what he did. "It is better to be thought a fool, than to open your mouth and _____!" Are you getting a clue?

From that day forward, he realized that when you are in your "suc-factor," you should not not prove it, but rather defer to those around you who are in their "success factor" – and then Performance Execution can only be the net result!

WOW! With the integration of only the first two Performance Execution ideas / technologies, greater efficiency and effectiveness can be attained by all. Imagine your self-talk now when considering doing anything: Does this play to my X-Factor, or, in-short, will I "suc" at this if I do it? When tasking others, you could simply ask, "Does this play to your X-Factor strength, or am I setting you up to 'suc'?"

Consider that this formula…

$$C = (T2+A+P+E+C)E2xR = R$$

Goes beyond EQ (the Attitude-driven variables also shaped by Experiences and Culture) and mere IQ (the Training variables also laid against the application of what you have performed, and thus accomplished, along with the Experience variables) to deliver a clear snapshot of what your PQ can become and is all about.

Organizations and associations must prepare individuals and hold individuals accountable to be VIPs. As presented earlier in this chapter, you should focus your energies first on your A level players, as these are your leaders, or the people with the capacity to be leaders. Then focus your same energies on your B level players, as any organization must have a back-fill of great contributors, workers, team members, and employees, and this is where you will find them!

Sequential developmental programs, experiences, jobs, interactions, certifications, etc. must be constantly evaluated to ensure they meet present needs and projected or forecasted future needs. By utilizing the **Player Capability Index**® diagnostic instrument, individuals can work more objectively and thoroughly in the direction of a greater PQ.

VIPs live for X-Factor development, continuous opportunities to showcase and apply their strength base, and they seemingly re-energize themselves by growing their and others' X-Factor base line through individual **Player Capability Index®** development – grow for it!

Remember, when you understand the **Player Capability Index®** of another person, you can practically forecast their actions and decisions!

Chapter Three

Truth Three:

USFx2x4® is Your Only Differentiator:

Identifying Your Uniqueness and Applying It for Success!

PQ Reality Check: An apple is no longer an apple...True Performance Execution stars do not compete with other forces; they make their own universe in which others compete with them!

Your universe is built and differentiated based upon one, or a combination of four unique forces on two parallel universes!

Let's explore the third truth of these six fundamental commonalities among every successful person, organization and enterprise which affords them the unique ability to deliver Performance Execution!

Third – The ability to attain peak performance and fluidly execute decisions is dependent upon being able to continuously make yourself (either personally or organizationally) relevant for the environment you are in and the market you serve. You are what you telegraph to others you are; thus, you can be more if you position yourself to be.

No one can be all things to all people all the time. Getting real with yourself and others is the only way to true Performance Execution behavior!

By grasping this next Performance Execution model, you can position yourself and your organization for even greater successes by being able to forecast what will be saleable in your future, i.e. read the market before it arrives.

As management guru Peter Drucker and others have famously proclaimed, the best way to predict your future is to create it, and with this model you can do just that!

In order to do this, however, you must continuously apply the **USFx2x4®** Model to yourself or your organization. It is important to recognize that all transactions of ownership revolve around this concept, and the applicability of it to everything you do to differentiate yourself from others is contingent upon this model. By recognizing that there are four psychological drivers to our decision process as consumers, you can always identify ways to ensure you are relevant and explore ways to continuously reinvent yourself for Performance Execution.

USFx2x4® is Your Only Differentiator
This drives what an individual's or organization's X-Factor should be!

Stop. Make sure you really read and understood the last sentence before continuing.

By applying the previous chapter's model to individuals, organizations, and the individual services or products each produces, you can then begin to determine what makes (or has the capacity to make) us great. With this USFx2x4 Model, you can discover just how to position yourself and others for Performance Execution.

Those who attain higher levels of Performance Execution (whether that is on an individual basis or organizationally) do so by first recognizing that the marketing world positions things (tangibles and intangibles) in the consumer's mind as either:

1. **Unique Selling Feature (USF #1)** – Which refers to all of the "WHAT Factors." What is it that you have to offer that no one else can match or surpass?

or

2. **Unique Service Feature (USF #2)** – Deals with all of the "HOW Factors" in the equation. How do you deliver your WHAT Factors that differentiate you from others?

Unique Selling and Service Features (USFx2) may also be called unique selling propositions by others – it's all the same.

With these two critical differentiators in diagnostically looking at yourself or others, you can begin to see why the level of execution with which you are associated is either exceeding expectations, acceptable, or a complete disaster.

With the understanding of USFx2, there are four fundamental ways to identify your uniqueness, (whether that be USF#1 or USF#2) or that of other individuals and organizations, and apply it for success. Psychology reveals that we position ourselves, we acquire something, we adapt to something, we adopt new behaviors, we change ourselves, or we resist a behavioral pattern for one of four reasons. Therefore, we can make the case that attaining a higher level of Performance Execution would be born out of recognizing which one(s) apply and exploiting them ruthlessly in pursuit of serving others.

Those who do, deliver!
Those who can't, talk a lot.
And those who want to, simply make it happen!

With the application of USF#1 and USF#2, you can evaluate what gives you a competitive advantage on one of four differentiating levels. These four differentiators are:

1. Better – The positioning of something / someone as better than what a marketplace knows about or has access to is always an inviting stimulus for consideration. Always be asking how you can be better at what you do, as that is your legacy. Then be continuously engaged in your own Human Capital development (IQ), interacting with winners around you to both learn from, and to raise your performance abilities (EQ), so that your ultimate output is always at an Olympic level (PQ).

2. Faster – Because multi-tasking, constant change, continuous demands upon us, and innovation are the trademarks of super-performers, identifying ways to increase efficiency without jeopardizing quality or brand equity is a non-negotiable aspect of the playing field today. Continuously seeking out ways to be more efficient (faster) is the new norm. This is, however, tempered by a realization that not every situation is the same, and thus, speed for speed's sake is also foolish for fool's sake!

3. Different – Enough said. All things being equal, you are equal. If you are equal, what is the leverage point or tipping point to encourage someone to continue connecting with you to attain greater performance? There isn't one! So, always be looking for ways to attain performance acceleration by recognizing that being different may be attractive and gain you a competitive advantage. Sometimes this may be something altogether new that the market has never experienced, or it can be a simple extension of an existing brand, service, or product.

4. Cost Effective / Cheaper – The bottom line is the bottom line. This does not mean that the lowest price always wins in the performance world or

with the Performance Executioner. When cost, price, investment, or the financials may, at first glance, be out of alignment with expectations, that is when the value proposition as justified by better / faster / different comes into play!

Want to test-drive these ideas to see how impactful they are and decide whether to project them to those with whom you interact?

Imagine yourself as a website, and hit print on every screen of who you are and what you would post as the 5Ws (who, what, when, where, why) and 1H (how) of yourself as You, Inc. Now take four different-colored highlighters, each one representing each of the "x4" differentiators.

1. Better = blue highlighter
2. Faster = yellow highlighter
3. Different = pink highlighter
4. Cost-effective = green highlighter

Go through every page of You, Inc. that has been printed, and as you read every word, highlight anything that speaks to the 5Ws or 1H. When you are done, if you are left with a lot of black ink on white paper and not much highlighted text, then you have just held yourself accountable, recognizing that you are not very unique – ouch!

If this is the case, you have fallen into the trap of what holds most back from attaining Performance Execution success. You have no USFs, nor do you posses much in the way of worthy X-Factor DNA – basically, you or your organization "SUC!"

You can apply this same matrix to your professional life. For example, make a printout of your organization's website, today's equivalent of your storefront on the cyber highway. On every printed page reflect on what text actually speaks to the above four USFx4 variables. The less that's said, or if what you do have spelled out is practically the same verbiage as what's on a competitor's website, then you do have an "apple-to-apple equivalent," and your longevity is in jeopardy, right now!

Performance Execution is about your USFx4 always being a little more or greatly enhanced in each of the four categories. When this is true, you are living your organizational X-Factor at the highest level of success.

Now want to see someone who understands this model? For decades, Detroit led the world in the automotive industry by bringing products to the marketplace that fed the consumer hunger of USFx2x4®. In fact, in 1971, do you know what the number-one-selling car model was in the world? How about the number-one car brand?

In 1971, the number one selling car model in the world was the Cutlass from the number-one car brand in the world, Oldsmobile, from the number-one automotive manufacturer in the world, General Motors. Today, the first two no longer exist, and the latter has long since lost its world dominance and position!

Complacency and self-centeredness by all players of management, labor unions, and consultants, slowly led them to become bottom feeders in the world market and watch as their market dominance became overtaken entirely by foreign manufacturers. This was not an accident. Now you know who was the first billion-dollar-a-year business in the world, now struggling to survive, on a daily basis!

When you have the blind leading the blind,
you should not be surprised when you drive directly into a wall of destruction!

I can clearly recall a conversation that occurred in 2004, while I was sitting in the office of a senior executive at Ford. On his desk was a brochure of a new Jaguar designed to capture the consumer attention of buyers of Mercedes, Lexus, Infinity, and Acura. The brochure had as impressive a look and feel as anything you would pick up at those premium brand dealerships. It truly surpassed the USF expected from anything presently being offered on the Ford or Jaguar lineup of 2004, and for that matter, Lexus, Infinity, or Acura as well.

When I asked how much the price point was, I was told it would be very competitive to the other brands, and that made it very attractive. As I reviewed the four color, multi-page brochure, I asked where the car was, and I was told that it was a "prototype" that would most likely not be available for several years.

That car showed up on the Ford and Jaguar dealership lots for consumers in 2009/2010 – years too late. And upon its arrival, it had no USF leverage in the market, but rather merely blended in once again! So sad.

What makes this Performance Execution implosion even worse is that by Spring 2009, based on Yahoo! and AOL seach engine welcome screens, that same model was rated to be the highest in customer complaints and the most repair-prone vehicle out that year – ouch! There is a USF media blast!

To compound how industry giants who once set records as Performance Execution stars can fall from grace when they take their eye off of the USFx2x4 ball, by late 2008 and early 2009, General Motors and Chrysler were in discussions about merging two failed businesses into one mega failure, and in 2010, the U.S. Government had to bail them out. Your X-Factor reveals your reality, or getting repeated government bailout subsidies.

As it announced its 100 year anniversary, General Motors wasn't doing great. In addition to announcing this landmark anniversary in 2008, it also announced an efficient, eco-friendly, multi-fuel car called the VOLT, to address market needs. The vehicle, however, would not be ready for the market until 2010. No wonder organizations and people continue to miss Performance Execution, play market follow-the-leader, and lose their previous market dominance!

Toyota, on the other hand, understands the USFx2x4 model and lives it. As the world's largest manufacturer of automobiles, it straddles the marketplace as a generational car company, making Toyota models for anyone between the ages of 16 and 100. It also recognizes that you can apply the USFx2x4 model to identify relevant emerging markets. That is why it makes a Toyota for all ages, a Lexus for the upscale and affluent middle aged, status-driven, materialistic demographic, and an adolescent car division for the youth market, called Scion. If you look at the design, color, label, position, price, advertising, market, sale, and support of each of these three divisions, it becomes obvious that the model of USFx2x4 is the same for each. The answers derived from the formula for each are the only things that differ!

Remember the ExpressJet examples detailed at the end of the last chapter, as this adds further perspective as to how the Player Capability Index and the USFx2x4 Model blend together and can assist you in attaining higher levels of Performance Execution.

For twenty years I have worked with differing state National Guard Adjutant Generals and their Recruiting and Retention Commanders. I have recognized a distinct performance curve that has developed with every state. Sometimes a state is a national leader at recruiting and retention, while other times each has been in dismal standings. One of the blatant reasons for this has been that individuals who grasp this specific Performance Execution step (having aligned mission statements with X-Factor participants assigned within each, and supported appropriately via the Player Capability Index) excel, while those who debate it, dismiss it, or focus disproportionately on other factors crash – every time!

From a Human Capital position, do not make the calculated mistake of positioning an individual within your organization just to be in alignment with some sort of a quota system or check list. If that individual does not truly have the X-Factor and Player Capability Index variables to be legitimate, nor the ability to enhance the team by bringing something better, different, faster (more efficient), or cost effective (financially worthy of their association), then do not make a long-term decision based upon a short-term need.

Jesse Jackson has made a very powerful diversity observation, that when organizations are truly aligned with individuals of not just differing ethnicitiy, but also of all gender, lifestyle, generational backgrounds, educational levels, etc., then, and only then, will an organization be able to experience how good a business can be.

By using a model like the Player Capability Index, Performance Execution can be attained at an even higher level. You can go beyond mere diversity inclusion as a Performance Execution advantage and attain "equanomics" – real equality and parity where inclusion of people of color on corporate boards, in senior leadership roles, advertising, and professional services can be quantified and measured.

Now, imagine that the Player Capability Index model were to be applied equally to all people, regardless of gender, ethnicity, or other differences. People would not be elevated if they did not have the credentials to be on the playing field, and there could be no more excuses in the new flattened global economy for exceptions – either you are a VIP, or you are a VUP!

Again, the power of this Performance Execution factor is that it allows for civility and rationalization to prevail in a world of emotions, hostility, and opinions. The application of this model makes conversations and decisions very straightforward, while increasing success attainment and decreasing self-imposed "suc" legacies.

The cancer to this PQ is that, in many organizations, affinity demographics or groups, governmental agencies, and cultures, we have created a world around us wherein there is no sense of urgency in what we deliver. People of VIP stature and mindset are expected to embrace, condone, tolerate, and even compensate people for:

1. Complacency in attitude and behavior
2. Resistance to embracing only VIP status in all you do
3. Apathy towards self-respect, self-worth, self-dignity, etc.
4. Personalization to a level of not assuming ownership

Warren Buffett has remarked on several occasions, when asked about some of his investing secrets over the decades, that while the balance sheets are important, he leaves a lot of that to his partner, who works out the details. He has long since recognized that what he looks for is a complete picture, and that the people factor to an organization in which he invests is essential to lasting and sustained success.

USA TODAY (1-14-2008) reported the Department of Transportation statistics (from 2002 through 2008) for total customer complaints with respect to the aviation industry and major airline carriers. Amazingly, American Airlines was rated number one during the entire run for most complaints filed. Does this mean they SUC? Probably not, but in one way of benchmarking SUCCESS, (their X-Factor) perception is king in the consumers mind. Do you think their leadership team grasps these first Three Models? Probably not (which begs additional macro performance execution questions at both the Board level and Senior Leadership level)! One way out of this abyss is the immediate application of the first Three Models and the implementation of the remaining Models. There are many exceptional AA / AMR team members, but for every ten VIPs, it only takes one VUP to nullify all their efforts.

I live in the Midwest, and I often take upwards of 20 or more flights per month. I have seen how the absence of performance standards and review systems can affect employees.

It is the internal self-esteem, self-worth, self-respect, self-pride, and self-professionalism that drives one person to exceptional levels of customer care, (as is the norm with the American Airlines team at Tulsa International Airport) while at the next airport (or the next flight crew experience) you would be excused for thinking you had just changed airlines completely!

Performance Execution is derived from an aggressive and ruthless understanding of how USFx2x4 can drive logic-based decisions and actions, as well as a sense of urgency in all you do. This allows you to truly shut down the emotion and prejudice that permeates those who "SUC!"

Chapter Four

Truth Four:

5 Integrated Mission Statements for Alignment and a Sense of Oneness:

Ensuring You and Others are Aligned to Not "Suc" is an Imperative for Survival at the Least and Ultimate Success as Your Endgame – Your Mental Action Plan for Success!

MAP: "Mental Action Plan"

Let's explore the fourth truth of these six fundamental commonalities among every successful person, organization and enterprise that affords them the unique ability to deliver Performance Execution!

Fourth – Building alignment with others and determining how best to integrate with other individuals and organizations can be driven through the understanding and sequential integration of Five Mission Statements. Understanding each mission statement, and how each mission statement chronologically influences one another, determines every choice you make or should not make, and how decisions are implemented among peak performers for efficient change and stress management. This subsequently reveals itself very clearly in productivity and profitability charts!

Alignment of multiple X-Factors brings individual people and competing business units together in harmony. Combined with market-appropriate USFs, this allows people to attain greater levels of success and sustainability in challenging times.

5 Integrated Mission Statements for Alignment

To ensure everyone's actions actually exhibit the actions that bring to life forward-moving mission statements, consider this organizations mission statement. It could easily be yours, and we will revisit it later:

"We are responsible for conducting [our] business affairs in accordance with all applicable laws and in a moral and honest manner... We want to be proud of [our company] and to know that it enjoys a reputation of fairness and honesty and that it is respected."

Never before have the five independent links been connected, and now they can accelerate greatness and serve as guideposts to find from where the cancers come which can derail you and others from attaining true Performance Execution greatness.

While working with the leadership teams at Anheuser-Busch Breweries, the new college graduate hires, and their aging senior employees, (what they call their "Matures") there became a need to integrate and work together more effectively. This model served as a guidepost for training immersion programs and duties assigned.

At the same time, while working with the entertainment teams of Sea World, this concept was spotlighted by a Senior HR Executive as having significant impact, exclaiming that their organization is dependent upon seasonal workers. Many of these seasonal workers are under the age of twenty-one, and it has been a repetitive challenge for decades to get everyone working in the same direction. A major factor is that people do not see the macro picture and how their micro sphere of responsibility contributes to or detracts from the winning formula!

It truly is this fourth component which is present with every successful person or organization who attains true success with managed, low, or no stress. Every action must be in alignment for ultimate X-Factor success to be actualized, and when this component does not exist, you can bank on the fact that you and others will "suc."

I offer a warning before reading this chapter. Understanding this fourth Performance Execution idea will render obsolete most unions and their previous advocates and will put the vocal minority to any cause on notice that viable solutions will be expected from them the next time they have a case of diatribe vomiting.

When an organization (however you wish to define that) has a sense of direction from a coherent set of sequential mission statements, each of which supports the others both vertically and horizontally, a sense of oneness develops. It is this sense of oneness that allows for diversity to be drawn upon, and for the assimilation of individuals into oneness to shine through and win. It is only when there is a sense of oneness that an organization can thrive and survive. (Go to *www.ThePerformanceMagazine.com* Volume 16 Issue 4 for a great column by former Colorado Governor Richard Lamm (D) on oneness and how it can kill America.)

When the oneness surrenders to the individuality of its members, that organization will no longer be capable of Performance Execution, and it will be its momentum in the market which will be the only factor allowing it to maintain temporary competitive advantage – it is like a slow-moving, killing cancer to an organization! Mission statements serve as more than just a MAP or an organization's and individual's guiding compass. They serve to represent what the reason for being is, and is not – oneness.

Southwest Airlines has understood this for more than three decades. In the past ten years, Harley-Davidson has learned the relevance of this in rebirthing their success, and so too have many others you will recognize at the end of this crucial model for allowing Performance Execution to take place!

The first and second of these models may seem clear, as academics for years have written, consulted, and preached about them. But because most of these strategists have never signed the front of a check, they lack the practitioner's ability to understand that there are three additional components to make the five mission statements actually produce success. Without them, it is only a matter of time before you will most surely "suc."

To ensure that you and others will assume ownership, work toward VICTORIES in a highly MOTIVATED way with PASSION, (reread Chapter One if necessary) and make sure that you and others are aligned with the five mission statements which sequentially interlink, one into the other, it is critical to understand who designs which mission statement and how they impact Performance Execution. The power of understanding these five mission statements also makes it easy to determine whether you have the X-Factor.

In reality, the reason most organizations don't survive today, (and even why family unity in America implodes at an alarming rate) is directly connected to a lack of understanding and adherence to these five mission statements. It is also due, in part, to people not aligning the five mission statements and integrating them with organizations – they should be assimilating them and having an operational expectation that others must align with them.

To gain alignment from all stakeholders to a larger unified enterprise, you MUST start at the macro level mission statement view, and work inward and downward. To accomplish this, people must have operational maps to guide what they do. In professional terms, this is called a mission statement.

To better understand the relevance of this concept, pretend you needed to drive from a known point to an unknown destination. You would most likely get a map or some sort of directions, correct? A mission statement serves the same purpose. It drives your every action and decision and ensures alignment to what you do. It also makes sure you draw upon the appropriate X-Factor in order to experience endless success destinations.

It is amazing how many people have no live MAPs or organizational mission statements to ensure Performance Execution. Then they wonder why they "suc."

Mission Statements serve as your MAP and guide you to success!

Here are the five sequential mission statements, each chronologically connected to the other:

1. **Mission Statement One: The Organization/ Enterprise/Family** – First, you must have the key stakeholders at the most senior level create the purpose of the entity. This drives all subsequent commitments, actions, behaviors, and decisions in which anyone and everyone will subsequently engage. The only people who participate here are the key individuals to that organization or family. Employees at large and children in general are not welcome here!

From this strategically-crafted macro statement, all subsequent decisions, actions, initiatives, programs, procedures, alliances, partnerships, outsourcing endeavors, etc. should be benchmarked. Anything you do must be in alignment with this mission statement, and if it is not, a serious conversation must take place immediately. If this is not addressed right away, the trajectory of the organization based upon micro outputs can be profoundly and adversely impacted.

2. **Mission Statement Two: The Subsequent Business Units (SBU, departments, teams, lines, shifts, etc.)** – Every entity or sub-entity that is necessary for the organization to deliver its goods (or services) is then created with strict alliance to Mission Statement One. In essence, how does

Mission Statement Two support Mission Statement One? The goal is that, once designed by the appropriate constituents and stakeholders, everyone can gauge their decisions and actions by it.

From this strategically-crafted statement, all subsequent decisions, actions, initiatives, programs, procedures, alliances you must execute, partnerships your drawn into, outsourcing endeavors you are subjected to, meetings and agendas you participate in, pet projects you deploy, etc. should be benchmarked. Anything you do must be in alignment with this mission statement, or the trajectory of the organization can be profoundly impacted.

3. **Mission Statement Three: The Constituent or End User** – Consider what you know about the entity, organization(s), or people you serve. Whether you serve a static constituent (internal or external customer) or multiple constituents, you must make sure that what you know about your constituents' needs and their purpose for existence has some alignment to yours, or the two of you will frequently be at odds on some level. Making sure that you attract constituents who align with who you are at mission statement levels one and two will breed greater success. By having this alignment, you will find that you will be at peace more often, and that you will be playing more often from your X-Factor baseline, which allows everyone to experience greater success!

Based on the previous two data statements, understanding the strategically-crafted statement of the constituent you are serving or seeking to serve, all subsequent decisions, actions, initiatives, programs, procedures, alliances, partnerships, out sourcing endeavors, etc. should be benchmarked. Anything you do must be in alignment with this mission statement, or the trajectory of the organization can be profoundly impacted.

4. **Mission Statement Four: Individual Colleagues Contributing to the Group Identity** – Here, the question becomes, do you know what the purpose or personal mission statement is of those co-workers within your organization, strategic business unit, department, entity (which could be further defined as your association, organization, church, group, family, etc.) that serve with you? At Mission Statement Four, you need to ask, "Do I know what drives each person in the organization?" It is completely acceptable that the answers may vary widely, but just knowing gives you the insight necessary to know how to align with them and how to assist them in aligning with others.

Each member of a team must be fully briefed on the previous three statements in detail to ensure they grasp them and are willing to embrace and align with them. If they are not, you have a deal breaker, and you should either work to synergistically get that person onboard with you, or terminate the relationship. Knowing the other person's statement then serves you in being able to forecast all subsequent decisions, actions, and initiatives they will engage in, and how that will impact their and others' trajectory towards Performance Execution.

5. **Mission Statement Five: Self** – At your core, what is your reason for being? What are your reasons for being a part of any and every organization with which you affiliate? For what do you stand, and for what do you not stand? A classic statement sheds light on this point, "If you do not know what you do and do not stand for, then you will stand for anything and everything." That will surely cause you eventual breakdown!

If you find that your personal mission statement is not in alignment with the preceding four, then you have two options to remain in balance and capable of Performance Execution: either change your Number Five to align with the first four, or change the first four to align with you. The answer to that question will reveal the obvious best solution for greater success.

With these MAPs clearly defined, you now have the capacity for greater insight into the mental action plans that will guide you and others to aligned success. You also have the insight to determine where potential tension and disconnect may arise.

Birds of a feather flock together…
A MAP tells everyone where to fly, and the absence of a MAP allows for misdirection in efforts!

The methodology to actually craft the words for any individual mission statement is really not a difficult science. From my experience working with and studying the most successful organizations for the past twenty-five years, I've noticed an individual mission statement needs only adhere to the 5W and 1H formula discussed earlier, in order to be successful. If, when a mission statement is read, each of the WHO, WHAT WHEN, WHERE, WHY and HOW are spoken to, then the opportunity for miscommunication, misunderstanding, assumptions, and missed expectations can be eliminated. This is an easy checklist to crafting a simple, concise, and sound mission statement.

In practically every peak-performing organization with which I work, study, or about which I learn from others, they have these MAPs clearly written out, designed at each level by only the appropriate stakeholders, and posted, from which everyone can benchmark their individual and collective efforts. They use these as road maps along the way in conversations, meeting management dynamics, agenda building, and strategic planning. Conversely, in nearly the same level of dysfunctional organizations and situations, there are either no MAPs (mission statements), or human interaction is adversely compounded by good people going off in different directions because each has different assumptions about what they believe the mission statement(s) to be.

While working with the Ritz-Carlton team in Naples, Florida, this theme of unity and success played out again. As I engaged a banquet staff member and asked a question about the set-up for a presentation I would be making to a group of C-Level officers to major business, she assumed total OWNERSHIP responsibility to find a solution and ensure that the solution provided by one of her colleagues was acceptable. When I inquired later about her level of alignment to the overall values of the organization, she produced from her pocket a business card size tri-fold that articulated the Ritz mission, which instantly informed her of her responsibilities: "Ladies and Gentlemen Serving Ladies and Gentlemen…You Own Any Concern or Problem Brought to You By a Guest" – WOW!

The next time you are on a Ritz-Carlton property or go by one, make it a Performance Execution field trip. Approach any member of the onsite team there and ask for a copy of their credo card. Observe how they light up and can produce one that they always carry. Ask them to explain some of the points about it and ways they are trained to live it. Every aspect is integrated into their purpose for existence – WOW!

Mission statements are like maps you would follow to drive from a known location to an unknown location. It amazes me how we all share a similarity in getting directions or having a map when driving a vehicle from a known location to an unknown location, yet people come to work and apply their energies in what they think is the correct direction, yet many never have a map to guide those actions and choices. Mission statements serve as your road map(s) to point your energies in the correct direction!

Many times it is not evident that people have not really been give their organization's or work unit's MAPs until it is evident that someone (or a group of people) are way off track. It is easier to get people re-aligned, (with far less stress and tension) when they are just a little bit off course. Once people have evolved far away from one another, realignment becomes significantly more challenging.

For example, imagine you were to take a dart board and place two differently-colored threads on the board. One color represents you, and the second represents the other person. Now pin your thread at the center bulls-eye to represent the starting point and stretch your thread outward to any other place on the board to represent your destination (goal, project deadlines, objectives, etc.). The next time you have a conflict in labor or activities, imagine where the other person would pull their thread (from the center bulls-eye) and pin it on the board to represent where they are. The space between the two threads is the gap between your MAPs and illustrates where the difference and break down in communication, expectations, etc. would be. More importantly, however, this off-track activity happened because the two of you were not in synch from the beginning. If both of you were clear on the final destination from the beginning, it would have been easier to recognize early on, any action being taken which, when extrapolated outward, would reveal if that action was congruent or incongruent with the final destination. That is how mission statement development and understanding works. It drives all actions in alignment with the thread, and ultimately, the end goal!

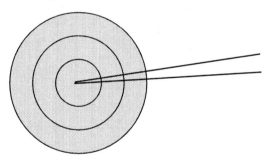

The next question for increased Performance Execution comes from how you can engage any group and generate **Centers of Influence** (COI), otherwise known as advocates, allies, or supporters. In your presence, these COIs rally toward your goals. In your absence, they ensure that no one becomes the spoiler and derails your game plans (by not allowing passive-aggressive behavior to exist). To ensure the alignment of Human Capital assets, and that everyone is going in the same direction, you must have advocates, allies, and key stakeholders in support of the mission statements.

At the outset of engaging any group, there are actually three subgroups which comprise the total group. It is important to understand that people are fluid, and while they may be in one subgroup, in one situation on any given day, if you change the (1) circumstances, or (2) individuals within a group, it may influence people to move among the three subgroups.

The power comes from understanding this basic model and applying it to everyone, every time, to give you the mental insight to understand who to engage first, second, and third, to build support and momentum. Madison Avenue, Hollywood, and politicians all greatly understand the implications of this model, and each invests significant resources in understanding how masses work and who the influencers of any group truly are – and they work them first, every time!

When looking at any group with which you interact, recognize at the outset that the individuals within any group fall into three subgroups - **Rule 80/10/10**™. It is your profile recognition of this dynamic which will empower you to attain greater success by determining with which subgroup to interface first, to build support. With their aid, they will bring along the masses. That combination will stifle the detractors every time. Consider:

1. Eighty percent of any group will be the people who have no real determining insight, nor will they take initiative. They are what I call the FOLLOWERS.

Anyone can become a follower for one of three fundamental reasons. By understanding why a particular person you have to engage is a follower, (in essence, by asking the right mental diagnostic question, the answer as to how to engage them becomes evident) you can then apply the antidote and engage them constructively.

People are followers for (1) legitimate reasons. Having never done or studied the issue at hand, they have no academic or practitioner mental action plan to guide their actions, therefore, the person shuts down until someone engages them and directs their actions – this can be either the transformer or the terrorist!

Another reason people may be followers is because they have been (2) forced into not being proactive and are waiting to see what the majority influence is before aligning themselves with that side.

Here, you need to engage and encourage them to become proactive and participate, thus aligning with you. If you do not enlist their participation, the terrorists will gladly do so!

The final reason someone becomes a follower is because (3) learned ambivalence allows them to escape participation because someone else will cover for them. Here, you just simply have to engage them directly so they begin to realize that, at least in your presence, you will hold them accountable.

2. Ten percent of any group will be the people who influence others in a forward, constructive manner, or what I call the TRANSFORMERS!

These are the people whose buy-in and support you can enlist to become your advocates, allies, and key stakeholders to influence others onward and forward with your MAPs. There are two fundamental ways to look at a group overall and determine within that group who the potential transformer prospects could be for you: (1) they could be any individual who likes you, who you tend to connect easily or best with, or who owes you a favor. If a person like this emerges, you want to pre-enlist them to your cause. Not knowing any of these individuals, you would then ask (2) who has the most to gain by your position or the issue you want to present to the overall group; implement profile analysis (age, ethnicity, gender, social and economic status, tenure, position/rank, education, profession, etc.) to arrive at your answer.

With the transformers on your side, when you walk into the group dynamic, you never put them on the spot, but you do name-drop their participation or support for what you present while you are presenting it. This pulls the group of followers in behind your cause and shuts down the terrorists.

3. Ten percent of any group at the outset may also always be the individuals who resist any idea or action that challenges their status quo. This usually happens for no sound reason other than they simply object and seem to fight anything and everything without ever providing a viable alternative course of action. These are your TERRORISTS!

You know a terrorist if you work for one, work with one, live with one, or gave birth to one. These people never have a logic-based, alternative action plan to a viable resolution or solution – all they know is how to find fault with everyone on everything!

Do you really think Tiger Woods drives a Buick on a regular basis as the 2008 GM Buick commercial which depicted him as their pitch man indicated? No, but it does not matter. The fact that Madison Avenue, on behalf of Detroit's GM, knows that buying patterns can be influenced by the right TRANSFORMER championing their cause, is all they care about.

"A house divided against itself cannot stand." Powerful words by President Abraham Lincoln. The integration of these MAPs as Mission Statements combined with buy-in from your TRANSFORMERS (as advocates) ensures greater Performance Execution!

With the right level of support behind you, and having everyone, at some level, in alignment with the overall, far-reaching mission statements, success is really the only viable option you can experience in life!

For 35 years (minus two business quarters) Southwest Airlines has been able to generate a profit, when no other American commercial airline even came close. How was this accomplished? Easy! Southwest Airlines created an organization and culture where OWNERSHIP was demonstrated at every level and with every individual. The organization's X-Factor drove their every action, and an individuals' Player Capability Index drove each person to participate; ensuring that every mission statement was achieved. In essence, they live the first three Performance Execution variables.

If you have ever patronized Southwest Airlines (and if not, ask someone who has), then you know it is not unusual to see the agent working the check-in counter at the front of the airport also working the gate. It is not unusual to see a gate agent take luggage or a baby stroller down the jet bridge stairs and hand it to a ramp colleague. Nor is it unusual to see a gate agent, or even a pilot, come aboard the plane and assist in cleaning the passenger cabin so the plane can be turned faster. Nor is it unusual to be on a plane which, after it lands, actually taxis to the gate at a fast speed. While this all serves as a norm at Southwest Airlines, it also serves as a rare occurrence with any other national airline, and therefore, a major clue as to why they are dysfunctional and not profitable. At Southwest everyone understands that if a plane is on the ground, it is losing money. If a plane is in the air, the company can be profitable. For that single, focused reason alone, everyone participates in profit sharing, and they each see how they contribute to the overall purpose of the business.

And while they are a union shop, notice that, unlike traditional union shops that condone laziness, insubordination and vandalism by their own members and employees, the employees of Southwest police themselves. Internal terrorists are a rare occurrence, and transformers are bred on a daily basis. The reason is that these professionals and individuals seek success instead of whining away in the "suc" zone of life!

Think of Mission Statements as a trajectory indicator. In working with the United Space Alliance / NASA for the past decade, I had the unique experience of suiting up and touring through the space shuttle ATLANTIS. As every child astronaut may recall, as the shuttle orbits in space, all you have to do is fire up the engines and barely touch the controls, and you can completely alter the trajectory with one sudden, yet little burst of energy. Mission statements to an organization, and to every member of that organization, serve to indicate which actions are in-bounds, and which are out-of-bounds in relation to what you do and its impact on where the mission statement indicates you are supposed to be heading!

Many interpersonal rivalries, turf wars, and conflicts center around individuals' micro beliefs and micro actions. To align everyone and their energies, mission statements serve to indicate the macro target so as to keep everyone on the correct trajectory!

Given the opportunity to come, people will come to you. Given the opportunity to leave, people will leave you. Given the opportunity to stay, people will stay! What opportunity do you provide to people?

Performance matters! Whether the performance is personal or professional, about you or those around you, performance today matters!

Paleontologist Stephen Jay Gould has made the case for growth, success, and performance advancement via his Theory of Punctuated Equilibrium, which suggests evolution doesn't happen at a slow, steady evolving rate, but rather in fast bursts over a long period of time.

Through years of working with top Fortune 500 companies, leading governmental organizations, successful non-profit organizations and associations, coupled with my interactions with some of the most powerful personalities through *Professional Performance Magazine*, I have seen other national publications come and go, businesses rise and fall, and individuals billed as great, disappear.

What we have recognized in all of this is the real differences between greatness and 'wannabe' greatness, is that successful people do the things that unsuccessful people do not. They do the fundamental work that is necessary, no matter how time consuming or difficult the tasks may be.

This could be an extension of Stephen Jay Gould's theory that I would call the Theory of Punctuated Performance Equilibrium. With it, all energies can be aligned for VIP accomplishments!

During the election cycle of 2007 through 2009, through the worst financial implosion in a century, America actually proved successful, contrary to the mainstream partisan media. Through the fall 2008 election cycle, proof positive that we are living in the hottest performance economy in more than ten years, the Small Business Administration (SBA) reported that more than 672,000 new companies with employees were created in 2007, an annual increase over the previous year, and a 12 percent increase over the Dot Com Boom. The Bureau of Labor Statistics adds that 6 percent unemployment is actually considered by the government to be a fully-employed American society. During the fall 2008 election cycle, unemployment statistics registered from 5.3 to 5.7 percent.

So what is the performance execution point? We may have just lived through the first completely media-manufactured election and financial crises. While 94 percent of Americans are actually solvent and making their mortgage payments in a timely manner, the media, and media-manufactured government of 2009 would report a world in crises (if you weighed in solely on the less-than-six-to-eight percent of irresponsible people who created their own nightmares).

Add to these performance trends (again, this is not a Democratic or Republican thing, but rather a performance thing – an American thing!) that 37 percent of these start-up individuals classify themselves in the highest tax bracket. Performance equilibrium is happening all around you! This is where true performers turn for the punctuated advantage!

After the American election of 2008, the unemployment statistics began to exceed the established six percent Federal guidepost for what is considered a fully-employed economy. What the financial shake-out started to reveal was that many businesses had positioned themselves to provide world-class crap for years, had overcompensated all of their employees (truth be told), and had overcharged for their goods.

It became clear that there was a need to deal with the realities of what the economy should never have tolerated: VUP wins occurring more often than VIP behaviors.

What mission statements and a firm sense of oneness reveal among every Performance Execution VIP is that mission statements:

1. Reinforce the sense and purpose for existence
2. Shape and drive culture
3. Drive values and behaviors
4. Reveal which performance standards will be measured and accepted, and what will be tolerated
5. Determine pride in organizations and self
6. Drive customers' perceptions and expectations of you

With these mission statements clearly defined, posted, and lived, by every performance participant from the front line to the top line, your MAPs will be clearly defined. If you do not have these, or allow them to be bought, bartered, and sold, you will stand for nothing!

Remember the mission statement example referenced at the beginning of this chapter? What happens when peoples' beliefs, thoughts, and real ACTIONS do not live up to their Mission Statement?

"We are responsible for conducting [our] business affairs in accordance with all applicable laws and in a moral and honest manner... We want to be proud of [our company] and to know that it enjoys a reputation of fairness and honesty and that it is respected."
- ENRON

Performance Execution is what differentiates those on the sidelines from those on the active playing fields. There are definite behaviors and characteristics of the greats. Here we will detail them for you.

Chapter Five

Truth Five:
The 4-Step STOP (decision making) Model Ends Complacency

If You Can't STOP to Make a Decision, Then There is No Decision to Execute!

Let's explore the fifth truth of these six fundamental commonalities among every successful person, organization and enterprise that affords them the unique ability to deliver Performance Execution!

Five – A major differentiator between those that achieve success and those on the sidelines of life in the "suc" zone, is the ability to make a decision (hence performance) and implement it (hence execution). Here you will recognize that personal preferences, personality styles, and social upbringing have hard-wired most people to innately be unable to make and facilitate decisions in a timely manner. Because of these variables, and many others, there is a four-step sequential decision model we created when working with IBM many years ago: the STOP Decision Analysis Model®. This sequential model provides you with a simplistic matrix to move forward and increase the output you strive for in your personal and professional life!

The 4-Step STOP Model Ends Complacency

Facilitating decisions comes down to understanding that the business brain only has four needs to be addressed and that there are, therefore, only four steps necessary to get from start to finish in a timely manner.

It is estimated that the top barriers to effective decision making in daily business run the gamut from procrastination and paralysis of analysis to fear and avoidance. Study any entrepreneur or individual perceived as successful, and what you will not observe is the presence of these barriers!

Successful people who grasp Performance Execution do one simple thing that all others do not... They execute performance!

Remember the study by the Conference Board referenced in Chapter Two as another perspective of why so many people do not execute decisions. Then, benchmark this next model against their behavior in order to determine how best to intervene with them. To learn that 71 percent of a demographic may very well be looking for a handout and not a hand up is simply cancer to Performance Execution.

Studies indicate that the level of risk associated with a decision, or the degree of risk created in a decision, can be predicted based upon your tendency to disproportionately focus too much energy in certain areas and not enough appropriate time in other areas of the decision process.

To increase your daily productivity, consider the basic functionality of how your brain processes data and how you can template that action for decision-making success.

In order to facilitate the basic process of decision making, your brain must:

1. See what the STIMULUS to be addressed is.
2. RATIONALIZE that stimulus as being worthy of your time.
3. Establish realistic paths of RECOURSE in dispensing with that stimulus.
4. With these viable recourse options in mind, be significantly more inclined to COMMIT to that recourse, which will then be made or implemented.

To facilitate the decision process in pursuit of increased productivity, and thus, profitability, to an organization or business, you need a decision-making formula that is easy, thorough and effective. The following formula is effective, in part, because it parallels the primary brain flow for making a decision from a business perspective. It also ensures avoidance of the barriers to effective decision-making. Consider the STOP Model:

1. **S: Stop and See** the stimulus at hand. If you can isolate and see WHAT the stimulus needing attention is, you will avoid procrastination. This means you are on your way toward increased productivity by avoiding the first barrier to success!

This phase is about clearly identifying WHAT it is that needs to be processed, acknowledging it, and moving forward. Here is where once you do recognize WHAT needs attention, you then accept the reality that there is no further reason to be making your point, presenting more data, continuing with more PowerPoint presentations, engaging in further conversation, etc.

Imagine the endless meetings by which you have previously been held hostage now coming to a non-combative conclusion, and the continued conversation transitioning to the next step in the four- step process!

2. **T: Target and Think** through WHY that stimulus has been brought to your attention. While you make a case for or against the stimulus, you are working through the rationalization phase. The second step to making or participating in the decision process is to make sure the rationalization, reasoning, and motivation factors are presented.

This is a critical phase and far too often overlooked by individuals in the workplace and home. By understanding the T step, you can begin to recognize patterns and trends, and work to change bad performance into healthy Performance Execution. People tend to forget to make the case for the S step, and that is what must take place here at the T step in order to get greater levels of buy-in and ownership, thus avoiding passive-aggressive counter energies.

By moving smoothly forward through this second step and recognizing that there is another step now into which to move, you will avoid paralysis of analysis, the second barrier to success!

3. **O: Organizing Options** for forward movement is the concentration of this third step in the decision process. Explore multiple viable recourses or option plans, recognizing that the word "options" in this step is plural. Until there are plural pathways, you should not hastily move forward.

By doing this, you can address fear-based reasons for not moving forward confidently, and become more confident to move to the fourth, and final step, in the decision process for increased productivity.

The beauty of this step is that, in interacting with others, it does not matter how applicable or outlandish others' ideas and action plans may be. You want multiple ideas presented on the virtual drawing board from which to select or combine synergistically for increased Performance Execution success!

4. **P: Pick, Preview, and Proceed** with the option that is most viable. By selecting the most viable option from step three and then committing to that action plan, Performance Execution is attained!

Should there be any degree of implementation problem, you will always have a backup plan. If, in-fact, you did step three effectively and not hastily, you will avoid the barrier of not moving forward. Program continual and regular review periods throughout the implementation phase to ensure that you are both on track, and allowing yourself to be open to lessons and opportunities. Then, if any adjustments become necessary, you can make them.

When conducting your reviews, re-run the four-step process as an endless loop, by continuously evaluating or re-evaluating any P, by imposing the S back upon it to ensure T indicates no need for alterations. Hence, O to what was implemented at P.

Understanding that your basic social style or personality style may make you predisposed to a comfort zone and willingness to spend more time in one of these steps than another, you must evolve through all four and let go of investing a disproportionate amount of time in any one step at the expense of the next and final step. A situation or vocational position may dictate that you spend more time in one step than another. But whatever the reality is, Performance Execution will only take place when you facilitate the chronological flow through all four steps!

The parallel applications of this formula are explosive. You can use it in pursuit of presentations and decision making with others. It facilitates a controlled, systematic dialogue, by presenting one item or step at a time. You will progress smoothly and increase group productivity.

Increased productivity comes from the basic functionality of the decision-making process. Gain this functionality by using the STOP Model daily!

This same application can be applied in designing teams, tasking out assignments, and cultivating the X-Factor within yourself and others.

The problem with a formula like this is that it makes very clear why some people "suc" and continue to "suc" long after a clear picture for success has revealed itself.

Use this STOP Formula as an overlay when watching television the next time journalists, commentators, politicians, labor activists, or any other impediment to Performance Execution are talking. Listen to see if they are hung up on denouncing someone else's P; yet if someone were to politely stop the conversation at that moment and ask (demand) that the person criticizing produce multiple viable alternative OPTIONS, could they? Would they? If they can, then you are dealing with a fellow Performance Execution star. But what you would hear most often if you attempted this is:

1. It is not my position to have a solution – WOW!

2. I asked you. It does not matter what I think – WOW!

3. We should form a committee to study this – WOW!

4. I have some ideas on this that we can talk about at another time – WOW!

Each of these are excuses for covering or masking the fact that they really are terrorists and do not possess the capacity to be transformers.

For example, for the first eight years after 9/11, the airline industry across the domestic United States market (minus Southwest Airlines) continued to find themselves not making enough money to pay their operational bills, let alone make a profit. Yet any traveling business professional in any major metropolitan city in America who ever sat in the back seat of a taxi had the opportunity to process via the STOP Model a sign staring them in the face that addressed their increasing operational expense issues (the rising price of fuel). "There is an $X surcharge for this ride, due to rising fuel costs." Amazingly, everyone understands what that message means, is willing to pay it, and no one bitches about it.

David Banmiller, the final CEO of Aloha Airlines, the 60-year-old Hawaiian airline that went out of business in 2008, attempted to save the firm by telling islanders (state political leaders, business owners, and traveling consumers) that the company had to charge a higher fee to cover their costs. But the state leadership of Hawaii did not intellectually grasp this, nor did their client base that insisted on fares like $29.95 for a route that should have been at least $100 plus. Two years after arriving to the company and preaching this new reality, the company ceased to exist – bankrupt and gone!

This is the same issue from 2003 through 2010 facing all domestic airline carriers in America. Simply run the four-step decision matrix, and the success plan is very simple. However, everyone wants to keep their heads in the sand and live in a world which prides itself on "suc" and make excuses for their positions. The solution to this comes with the O step of the STOP Formula. One such idea would be to simply add a fuel surcharge to every seat by taking the increased fuel charge and dividing it out across every seat equally. There you have the answer.

This sequential model provides you a simplistic matrix to move forward and increase the Performance Execution output you strive for in your personal and professional life!

The number of people wasting space on this planet by talking about doing things and yet never executing anything is limitless – just listen to any politician make the case for another committee to study something. Never do they offer a solution to doing anything. The same holds true for business leaders, colleagues, neighbors, and probably members of your own family tree!

Here are a few clues that you are stuck, and straightforward, simple solutions for each:

1. Procrastination – The inability to Stop and See WHAT you need to deal with. In many situations today, individuals and business units have learned to play brain dead so they do not have to address their realities. Worse yet, by avoiding the identification of needs, people can also abdicate responsibility and not have to assume Ownership.

If the **Player Capability Index**® is inappropriately applied by an organization or individual, then you may also experience people in command and control or influence positions that should be facilitating this model, but procrastinate unwittingly because they have surrounded themselves with people who have no clue about short-term actions and their impact upon long-term realities.

Here is a clue: if you cannot apply the first step, then step off the planet – you are taking up space for someone wanting to contribute!

The more amiable a personality you are, or the more you have previously been belittled for being proactive, the more likely you tend to get bogged down.

2. Paralysis of Analysis – The comfort zone or ability to target a stimulus and think through it for extended periods of time, a desire to form another committee or team to further study what someone else has studied, analyzing from habit, looking for one more reference data point, building excel spreadsheets and PowerPoint presentations to make your case…Here's a clue: if you have more than one data point to make your case as to WHY you have raised WHAT you have, then you're done   move onward!

Whether you are more of a linear thinker or an analytical one, this becomes your comfort zone, and this is where you tend to get bogged down.

3. Fear – The concern that, from a multitude of options that have been organized on focusing HOW to address the identified stimulus, you still cannot progress onward and forward for fear of failure, fear of not having enough data to make a sound decision, fear of the ramifications of an implemented solution, etc. Get over it! With at least two viable options on the table, it is time to move onward to the final step in making and implementing decisions. Should something go wrong, you already have a backup plan. No plan is ever perfect, but there are always viable plans for execution!

The more expressive or more social you are, the more you probably like to operate in a more consensus or collaborative way, and this is where you tend to get bogged down.

Performance Execution is the natural progression of these four decision process steps, culminating in the final stage of picking a viable option and proceeding with it!

I am reminded of a classic line attributed to the late General George S. Patton, who said, "Tell people what you want (P) and let them impress you with their ingenuity (Os that will feed P)!"

As you elevate your performance to a global economy, where people play in both the real-time world and virtual world, your ability to manage yourself and build enterprises whereby others do not have to be micro-managed and can facilitate this model by themselves will result in Performance Execution becoming attainable by all. WOW! Imagine a world where people can actually think independently, and can make and implement a decision.

Chapter Six

Truth Six:

Your Mental Teeter-Totter® Directly Impacts Your Self Talk and
Mental Life Balance – Period!

PQ Reality Check: *You are not what you eat...*
You are what you say you are!

Inventorying the voices in your head (and the voices you allow into your head) determines the level of Performance Execution you and others can attain!

Let's explore the sixth truth of these six fundamental commonalities among every successful person, organization and enterprise today that affords them the unique ability to deliver Performance Execution!

Six – We are the sum whole of every influence we have allowed, or unwittingly allowed into our subconscious mind, which actively or passively tells us how to assess every situation, encounter, person, and opportunity. Performance Execution comes down to accessing the constructive influences while objectively assessing and compartmentalizing the negatives.

Whether you read about Performance Execution Tour d'France star Lance Armstrong from birth to present day, or golf phenomenon Tiger Woods, Warren Buffett or Suze Orman, what each has in common is what occupies their mental teeter-totter, as it directly impacts their self-talk and mental life balance.

Your Mental Teeter-Totter® Directly Impacts Your Self-Talk and Mental Life Balance – Period!

Think of it this way. Visualize a teeter-totter (like a weighing scale) as if it were depicted as a flat panel screen on your forehead. As you look into a virtual mirror at yourself, one side of the teeter-totter contains all of the positive (PLUS SIGN / +), constructive, nurturing influences.

These serve as voices to you whenever you consider doing or saying anything. They are processed in a nanosecond, and are reflected in what you say or do out loud.

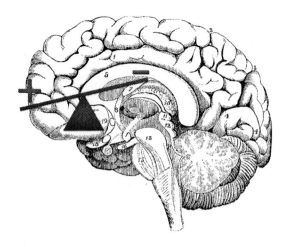

Conversely, the other side of the teeter-totter represents all of the negative (NEGATIVE SIGN / -), destructive, counter, whining influences.

These serve as voices to you whenever you consider doing or saying anything. They are processed in a nanosecond, and are reflected in what you say or do out loud.

The side of the teeter-totter which is weighed down more within an individual, organization, or group, over-influences the lack of performance or Performance Execution one will experience. In order to clarify how this works, imagine the brain from a business perspective rather than a medical perspective.

The front left side of the diagram represents the frontal section of the performance brain, known as the neocortex. It serves like the job description for a position in an organization that:

1. Processes new data
2. Serves as the learning center of the brain

Visually, you can recognize this space as the smaller of the two sides. The back-side, or right side in the above diagram is significantly larger, and the Performance Execution star understands and manages this accordingly. Stanford University has volumes of data on brainwave management and suggests that what we use as front side, conscious brain energy is merely six to seventeen percent of our brain matter. When you daydream, this section is off, when you sleep it is off, and when you are dead it is off.

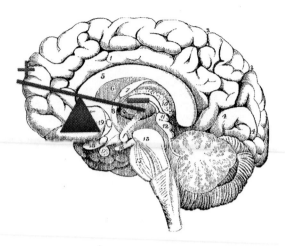

A better question in looking at those who do not play to their X-Factor, refuse to grow their Player Capability Index®, resist exploring innovative USFx2x4® factors, and deviate from the 5 Integrated Mission Statements would be, "How often is it on?"

The back right side of the diagram represents the rear section of the performance brain, known as the limbic system. It serves like the job description for a position in an organization, where:

1. Memories are stored
2. Habits radiate outward
3. Emotions are birthed

What we draw upon to guide our behaviors is the larger right or back-side. Imagine the computer adage, "Garbage in, garbage out." This is how the teeter-totter concept can guide your performance levels both in the present tense and for future efforts. Conversely, if you know what occupies an individual's or organization's teeter-totter, you can forecast actions – Performance Execution!

If a person has disproportionately more "suc-factors" on their teeter-totter, (which represents the totality of what is in the back right side area of the brain) then lack of Performance Execution will be the reality. If there are more positives, then Performance Execution success will be attained – the limbic system is the key.

Imagine individuals and organizations which play to the terrorists and not the transformers, individuals and organizations which resist Performance Execution at the highest levels, and individuals and organizations which want to participate in their future based upon past-tense teeter-totter variables, instead of seeking out new performance influences.

More often than not, (to ensure overall Performance Execution success) your teeter-totter is comprised of influences (from birth to death) from nine life-balance areas. I call this your PFC FISHES model. You can begin to inventory which influences may consciously or subconsciously be on your teeter-totter, or anyone else's, by recognizing what you know about their life influences from the following specific areas:

1. Professional aspects
2. Family aspects
3. Community aspects and interactions
4. Financial aspects, past and present tense
5. Inspirational aspects
6. Social aspects
7. Health and fitness aspects
8. Educational, knowledge, and training aspects
9. Spiritual aspects

When I reflect back over this matrix, a memory comes in to my mind from childhood (FAMILY) that still has an influence upon my Performance Execution DNA today. Getting off the school bus, finishing my childhood chores on our pig farm, and getting out my HotWheels® and playing with them in the dirt pile adjacent to the pig barn, was a childhood highlight. Now, if you have ever been on a farm, you can imagine what the dirt pile really was, but when you're a child, you don't see the crap – you just see the fun!

Every job has a crap quotient.
Performance Execution is about working through that, and realizing that there is also a success quotient!

Another moment that had a profound Performance Execution influence on my DNA was when my high school cross-country coach, Graeme Badger (EDUCATION), advised me to attend an out-of-state college upon graduation. He noted that in his twenty years of high school teaching he had noticed that every student that left the state for college grew significantly further in

Performance Execution stature than what he observed as the norm of every student that stayed in-state to attend college. His point was not that an in-state school would be bad for me, it was:

1. Pick a college so far away geographically that you can't easily get home every weekend...

2. Pick a college where you will be forced to stand on your own and not be able to rely upon any of the structures or people you have if you stayed home...

3. Pick a college where, ideally, you do not know anyone, and then you can make your own choices with no teeter-totter guilt or preconceived expectations...

4. If you really want to see what Performance Execution possibilities lie dormant within you, go somewhere outside of your teeter-totter norm!

People with authority typically surround themselves with confidantes and those they feel should be groomed for roles containing increased levels of responsibility.

After surveying the CEOs, CFOs, and CLOs (Chief Learning Officer) of the top businesses in America for the past decade, I have discovered that these influential individuals are continuously feeding their mental teeter-totters more positive stimuli than negative.

Bet on the BETA (brains, energy, talent, attitude) Factor® for Self-Development Effectiveness & Market Advantage for Your Mental Teeter-Totter!

Performance Execution stars look for four specific qualities within those they associate with and the influences that they feed into their mental teeter-totter, knowing that these variables have a direct correlation on their Performance Execution output. The best-of-the-best would coach you to continuously increase your exposure to the nine PFC FISHES aspects of life, which feed into a Performance Execution stars' BETA Factor®:

1. **Brains.** Do you have the formal and informal educational foundation that success requires? What degrees, citations, certifications, and other trainings have you acquired? Are you qualified for the position right now, or do

you need additional training to succeed? What is the totality of available technical and non-technical education for your X-Factors if the B were applied to it? What percentage of the universe do you possess, and what percentage do you actively seek?

2. **Energy.** Can you hold up to the rigors of the position from both a mental and physical perspective? Is your reputation within the organization such that your colleagues recognize you as a person who continually exhibits stamina, energy, initiative, dedication, creative juice, and diligence? Is your reputation rooted in quantifiable records, present assignments and future possibilities? Do you find yourself having to force yourself to go to bed at night, and do you find that you awake before the alarm clock goes off in the mornings, primarily due to your energized state of mind for who you are and what you are doing? That is pure Performance Execution!

3. **Talent.** Do you consider yourself an accomplished colleague both from an individual and team perspective? In other words, do you have a record of personal accomplishments and team accomplishments? Do you frequently snub team interaction and decision-making opportunities because you would rather pursue assignments where you individually, reap the rewards? Talent is presented for others' gains as well – not just yours!

4. **Attitude.** You have absolute control over one factor in life: your attitude. What does your attitude telegraph to those around you? Do you have a positive or negative attitude? What do others think? The first two aspects of the BETA Factor – brains and energy – can be cultivated and honed. Attitude is such a core element that it is almost impossible to significantly alter it for long periods of time. Very few can actually fabricate a positive and healthy attitude.

An alarming organizational fact is that many personnel within an organization understand what it takes to move the organization forward, yet they pursue positions and promotions that are less than their X-Factors. They are not honestly representing their capabilities because they are too consumed with the promotional possibilities from a selfish perspective. This only penalizes the organization and its talented members. It is the leader's responsibility to ensure that the organization deliberately develops the BETA Factor° of its employees, and promotes only those who sincerely demonstrate their proven BETA abilities.

What you load onto your mental teeter-totter, and with whom you mentally surround yourself, directly influences who you are and what you can achieve!

Forget the press headlines, the fashionable psychobabble of the day, and the latest pop book from a neo-nothing. The reality is that we all have the same base ingredients that can lead to Performance Execution success, mediocrity, or failure – the DNA called YOU. And now, you can inventory your mental teeter-totter.

Regardless of the date on your driver's license or the inner age of your heart and soul, your comfort zone and level of what you are willing to tolerate, directly drives your reality – good or bad. Throughout my career, I, like you, have had the opportunity to meet a wide spectrum of people, and every achiever I have encountered has one common characteristic. They have a clear understanding of this internal mental teeter-totter concept, and when it comes to the people they allow onto it, it becomes a very-clearly-defined roster of critical influences that occupy their minds.

This mental teeter-totter serves as a sort of mental Board of Directors to influence precisely how they see themselves and which voices talk to them at any given time.

Birds of a feather flock together…
Inventory your mental teeter-totter to see with whom you have been flying, and recognize with whom you will soar in the future!

We have established the fact that this teeter-totter of multiple influences drives your conscious (being proactive and responsive) and, in many cases, unfortunately, your unconscious (being reactive and emotional) thought processes, which drive your judgments and dictate your behaviors!

The dominant influences on your teeter-totter are the people on it. To better understand the people around you today, and especially when interacting with the different generational segmentations in your professional life, start asking which influences (time, geography, people, experiences, places, responsibilities, social, entertainment, etc.) are in your head, and better yet, in someone else's. (For more on generational segmentations in society today and how understanding how to attain peak Performance Execution from each will truly be your success differentiator of tomorrow, read Appendix Two in this book.)

I have recognized that peak achievers and high-potential individuals (high-po) maintain, at a minimum, very specific types of "people" in their life. These people (influences) may be comprised of individuals who have passed away, past interactions, or a present physical connection which you have today, all serving as internal mental drivers of how you:

1. See yourself
2. Measure yourself
3. Benchmark yourself against your true internal, physical, and mental abilities
4. Conduct internal discussions
5. Manage yourself
6. Outwardly engage others

"Garbage in, garbage out," could be applied to this segmentation of the teeter-totter specifically in evaluating how you operate. To see precisely how this common characteristic can be harnessed for constructive forward-life performance (personal and professional), I would ask you to participate in a quick mental exercise.

If you do, in fact, see that there is a finite list of people, (past tense or present tense) that occupy real estate in your head and influence how you think and feel, then flex open the palm of your hand. Now, with the five fingers exposed, assign one name from this mental Board of Directors to one finger and do a countdown to quickly inventory just how many people immediately come to mind.

These mental names may be a family member or an extended family member. They may be a friend, co-worker, or your elementary school teacher.

As you conduct this simple exercise, recognize how many fingers become collapsed down. For most people, this exercise yields about five immediate names, and your flexed open hand becomes transformed into a fist. I refer to this mental Board of Directors concept as your FIST Factor™, and it represents where you get your internal power, strength, and energy – or lack thereof!

Just as the fist took a symbolism in the 1960s of power, strength, and energy, so, too, can you recognize what you have either chosen, or passively allowed others to do by infiltrating your thinking patterns. These people either play a part in your power, strength, and energy, or serve as terrorists to you and deplete these necessities. Smart people genuinely engage others in pursuit of service to themselves and others, while shrewd people may appear to have a powerful network, but underneath they are very self-serving and will use you to gain anything for themselves, regardless of the implication upon others. This is also revealed if you dig deep to see who a person really has as their life influences on the teeter-totter – WOW!

Your teeter-totter becomes your FIST Factor™ – you do choose your reality.

Think of your FIST Factor as your own personal Board of Directors. These individuals can be engaged at-will for perspective and guidance to better increase your success ratios in life. Inventory whether your FIST Factor™, or mental Board of Directors, is serving you well or hindering your potential. There are five distinct types of individuals you want in your head for active, conscious access. If any of these categories is missing, it is time to seek out a new member. You may also recognize, when you evaluate this list and benchmark it against the present members in your head, that you may be lopsided and can gain better balance by replacing one or more members.

A balanced FIST Factor should have representation in the following five categories:

1. Family Member – Understands who you are
2. Friend – Knows what you can be
3. Professional Peer – Understands your vocation and occupational realities
4. Success – The single-most successful person you actually know
5. Underdog – The person who faces adversity and challenges, yet never gives up

If you have a terrorist in your head, it is time to "fire them" and consciously, actively replace them with someone who is a tangible contributor to success and achievement!

To ensure that you realize how important these people are, remind yourself of the five categories of the FIST Factor makeup. Recognize that these teeter-totter influences can change very slightly without you realizing it, yet they can yield a significant trajectory change on your life, or that of others.

Consider:

1. Look back one year ago on the calendar and ask yourself: where you lived, what you did professionally, and where you shopped for groceries on a regular basis.

2. As a reference point with these three series of questions, look and determine if there are any new mental faces you have seen in the past year?

3. Now ask the same question, but go back ten years.

4. Do you see any changes?

5. The point is simple. If you make a major life change and are not attentive to it, it may also change the makeup of your mental influences – garbage in, garbage out!

Increase your performance interaction ability with others by considering what references you know in advance when you engage a person. Generational diversity, ethnicity, gender, and gender bias are all shaped by your teeter-totter and the people who make up your FIST Factor!

Based upon your generational age group, (for simplicity, just use age groupings for every decade – are you in your 20s, 30s, 40s, 50s, 60s, etc.?) notice what voices are in your head which would qualify as healthy proactive voices. Then reflect on generational segmentations younger than you to determine what they may be carrying.

Most of us try not to act sexist, (gender neutral) or racist, (ethnicity neutral) but we do not realize the diversity of generational segmentations, and how our self-talk may be the most powerful future asset to outward success and interaction. Make sure your mental state has constructive reference points for engaging others of any age, gender, or color, for maximum positive self-talk and outward interaction. Then elevate your performance by recognizing that while you have an overall FIST Factor for You, Inc., you could also have temporary, specific FIST Factors to mentally guide you to even greater performance feats on a cause-by-cause, situation-by-situation, project-by-project basis. Here, you mentally pull up only those archived names and past experiences which would cause you to make better decisions and put forth the best behaviors.

Performance Execution of organizations can be weighed against this same variable. Look at the complexion of any team and ask yourself what you know about each person's teeter-totter and the makeup of influences within each person's head. Remember the flat panel screen referenced earlier, and determine which way each individual's teeter-totters are leaning – this gives you a pretty good clue as to how they conduct themselves!

Consider that for nearly fifty years, one individual alone had influence and gave counsel to Presidents Eisenhower, Kennedy, Johnson, Nixon, Ford, Carter, Reagan, Bush (senior), and Clinton: the Reverend Billy Graham. Consider the generational perspective and intense teeter-totter of influences he possessed, and was able to draw upon for the benefit of others.

Now consider that one couple has had the ear and counsel of Presidents Reagan, Bush (senior), Clinton, Bush (W), and the next President: James Carville and Mary Matalin. Consider their generational perspective, and their teeter-totter of influences that they are able to draw upon for the benefit of others (see www. ThePerformanceMagazine.com Volume 16, Edition 4 for a feature column with their Performance Execution thoughts for Americans).

You choose your reality as an individual, and you choose your reality as a professional. With whom you mentally surround yourself directly influences who you are and what you can achieve!

With rare exception, you can take an individual out of bad circumstances, but that does not mean you can take the bad circumstances out of the individual. Once that operational DNA of a person or organization is planted within someone's teeter-totter, it is hard to erase or override, but it can be managed away.

The reality is that when you observe a nation, civilization, organization, or individual, and understand (which does not mean you have to agree) what is on their mental teeter-totter, and what they see as the prospects for the future, (items, people, influences to be added to their teeter-totter) you can now forecast with relatively high accuracy their behaviors in the immediate future.

Every group and every individual telegraphs their teeter-totter. To measure where a person's teeter-totter is leaning, you will need to consider:

1. Facial gestures
2. Dress
3. Posture
4. Behaviors
5. Tone of voice
6. Word choice
7. How they engage others
8. Whether they can interact one-on-one or need a support group (fan club)
9. Etc.

The sad reality is that more people can easier see how to "suc" than how to "succeed," and society has arrived at a place wherein we condone this status quo.

Performance Execution within organizations and from our leaders must be elevated to the level of applying these six Performance Execution factors to others, and more importantly, ruthlessly demanding that individuals play by them today, and in our future, for sustained health and well-being.
Those who recognize the power of the mental teeter-totter and the critical nature of what is placed onto it, will allow themselves to remain true VIPs and be able to elevate others to Performance Execution greatness!

All too often, however, we have created a world wherein people play (and are allowed to play) the victim, and others continuously rescue them because they live and die by their very own "suc-factor" reality. Yet, they do not see, nor can they intellectually comprehend, that while their IQ fades, their EQ is electrified, and their PQ does not exist! Yet all along, they feed their mental teeter-totters continuous negative influences and reinforcement. So they really are VUPs who people continue to tolerate, do not hold accountable, or demand that they, too, step outside their own pathetic level of contribution and become VIPs if they wish to be treated, compensated, and recognized as VIPs!

In many situations you now can apply the teeter-totter model when you engage another person, interact with another group, or merge business units together. Realize that the first agenda item in many situations may be to neutralize the other party's teeter-totter before you can engage in a constructive manner for X-Factor success.

VIPs have the innate ability to start with neutral teeter-totter placement internally and with others. For that reason, their agendas are more widely

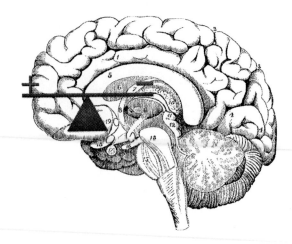

embraced, and Performance Execution is attained more efficiently and effectively!

Ultimately, the teeter-totter an individual or organization posses, reinforces, and builds upon will:

1. Reinforce their sense and purpose for existence
2. Shape and drive their personality, character, and reputation
3. Drive values and behaviors
4. Reveal which performance standards will be measured and accepted and what will be tolerated
5. Determine self-pride, self-respect, self-dignity, self-worth, and self-belief
6. Drive others' perceptions and expectations

What does your teeter-totter reveal about you?

Conclusion

Stand Up, Shut Up & Take Ownership

The foundation stage to pure Performance Execution success, which with we started in Chapter Zero, is where we conclude. Every person, parent, colleague, and employer struggles daily with why most people abdicate responsibility and only a few assume OWNERSHIP (of a cause, project, activity, situation, job, etc.).

So again, let's conclude by re-exploring how these six fundamental truths or commonalities among every successful person, organization and enterprise today and tomorrow emerge. It is these commonalities that afford them the unique ability to deliver Performance Execution!

Stand Up, Shut Up & Take Ownership

Performance Execution starts and ends with setting yourself (and others) up for pure success. To do this, you must understand the four cornerstones of the Ownership Model. Ensuring success and the drivers to ownership comes down to the victories you have and can experience repeatedly.

"Take ownership, control your destiny!
Blame others, live in infamy!"

Repeatedly creating climates whereby individuals assume ownership of their actions, tasks, and the reputation of an organization comes down to a simple sequence of interlinked actions. In working with for-profit and not-for-profit organizations over the past decade, a clear model has risen that differentiates the winners from the losers – those who are successful versus those who "suc".

One of the undisputed global business success stories and standout leaders of the past decade was that of A.G. Lafley, CEO of Proctor & Gamble (P&G). In the first decade of this century he has made this exceedingly evident by reshaping a global consumer products organization into an even greater brand. "The best way to drive success is to innovate… sustained organic growth!" Lafley says. In creating this winning organization whereby everyone rises to the level of owning their sphere of influence, "individuals execute when individuals have a sense of fearlessness when it comes to failure!"

As the CEO, he has assumed ownership and spun off $100-million-dollar business products and units that could not make their business model success ratios. Others in the business world would have been pleased with such profits based upon micro vision and immediate gains, but here, ownership dictates that you must maintain a macro perspective and big picture needs.

Whether in the executive suite, the frontline, or assembly line, winning Performance Execution stars understand how VICTORY breeds OWNERSHIP. The alignment of the Six Fundamental Commonalities presented in this book spell your secret to success.

Robert "Steve" Miller, former CEO and turn around guru to Aetna, Morrison-Knudson, Waste Management, Bethlehem Steel, and Delphi Corp., received his early training as a rising star within Ford, and later, side-by-side with Lee Iacocca as they saved and turned around Chrysler!

Serving on the boards of top organizations today, Miller is very clear on Performance Execution at the CEO level. A page from which we can all learn something – organizations which follow these tenants tend to prosper.

He has been quoted widely as saying, when a CEO cannot make a profit after four or five quarters, either he or she "does not know something is

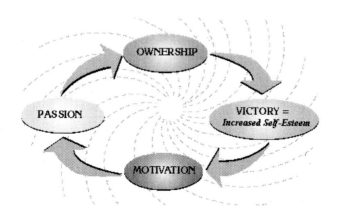

fundamentally wrong, or knows it, but refuses to acknowledge it." That means they are failing to assume OWNERSHIP and lack the PASSION or MOTIVATION to do what they have been entrusted to do!

One more time, winning organizations and individuals assume ownership, and do not engage in the excuse game for not attaining performance expectations. How you go about assuming ownership, and how you go about creating a climate wherein others assume ownership of their jobs, responsibilities, themselves, and the organization overall can be achieved by understanding how four factors are interlinked, and thus, where your first energies must be directed.

The burning question in the mind of most individuals is, "How do we go about getting others to assume a higher level of ownership?" With this question in mind, I began my homework assignment. What I learned is:

1. When you know what the depth of your skill abilities (formal and informal education, technical and non-technical training, certification and credentialed work, accolade experiences) is, and you draw upon those and apply them appropriately, you experience success and accomplishment or a self-VICTORY. When you experience a VICTORY, your self-esteem goes up!

The same then holds to be true in your engagement of others.

2. When you are victorious, you become significantly more MOTIVATED to apply yourself and assume more responsibility and you become more excited about participating. At this point, the necessity to establish incentive and motivation programs becomes less necessary!

3. When you become motivated from seeing your victories and successes, you become significantly more PASSIONATE about life and the endeavors you apply yourself to.

4. We take OWNERSHIP of those things and people about which we are passionate.

5. To get people to take more ownership, set them up for VICTORY!

I did reverse analysis of some of the most successful businesses, many of whom are my own clients today (Harley-Davidson, Army National Guard,

Walmart, Boeing, Target, Anheuser-Busch, SeaWorld, Southwest Airlines, and many more) and found that Performance Execution is about accomplishing meaningful outcomes. To do this, the starting point is not ownership issues at all, but rather setting yourself up for victories and success.

Owners own ownership.
Losers lose and own that!

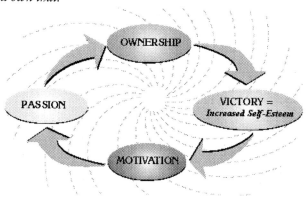

Look at the model again, and realize that to make the model move forward, the starting point is VICTORY; which always puts performance in motion for execution.

People who assume OWNERSHIP seem to be among the most PASSIONATE for what they do. Those who have high passion for what they do are continuously MOTIVATED by what they do. This only happens when people are set up for VICTORIES by doing those things which they are best mentally and physically equipped to undertake. All of this feeds their self-esteem. When you operate from a level of high self-esteem, it is both exciting to see what you can accomplish and also reveals of what you are willing to assume OWNERSHIP!

Remember the cult-like business followership of associations and businesses to Jim Collins' classic book *Good to Great*. He used the bus as a metaphor for leadership teams and indicated that success, and thus, avoidance of "suc" are about getting the right people on your bus, the wrong ones off your bus, and the remaining players on the bus in the right place. The bus could be expanded to be an entire group or an individual's way of seeing themselves and what they should, or should not do.

For you to attain greater levels of success, and sustained levels of success, you first must shed some mental childhood DNA, as most people today play from a mental reference that almost assures that they "suc".

Want to know what I mean? Think about how many times you have heard or told someone:

1. Identify what you are good at in life and always be looking for opportunities to apply yourself there. Heard that line before? If so, continue with that level of operation – **this breeds success!**

2. Identify what you are good at, and recognize what you are weak at. Then, when you find yourself having to do something that is not a strength, you can draw upon some of your strengths to compliment your weaknesses and most likely prevail and be successful. Heard that line before? If so, continue with that level of operation – **this breeds success!**

3. Identify what your core or net weaknesses are and then apply yourself and work to overcome them. Heard that line before? If so, do not continue with that level of operation, or you will most assuredly "suc" for life!

When a person experiences a lack of VICTORIES, look at what that does to their MOTIVATION. With that answer, ask what that does to their PASSION. With that answer, it becomes very clear why people do not want to assume more OWNERSHIP of the situations, activities, projects, or jobs that continue to set them up to "suc"!

Either you are an active participant in the problem,
or you are an active participant in the solution!
Either way you are taking an ownership stake and participating!

Need an example? There was a gentleman who lived in Chicago and played a little NBA. He became known by most measurements as someone who excelled at professional basketball, set all the records, and had the attention and respect of Madison Avenue and Main Street, USA. Then he tried his hand at professional baseball. It did not take him nor anyone else very long to realize that at basketball he was an undisputed success, while at baseball he "suc"-ed. According to the above logic, he followed one and two, and abdicated number three. Who was this person? Michael Jordan.

Why do children and adults abdicate taking ownership of what people expect them to do, or why do you seem to shy away from excitedly taking control of something and executing it to a high level of performance success? It is because of three factors directly taken from the preceding diagram:

1. We tend not to volunteer or sign up for endeavors which do not play to our abilities, which drive us toward non-victories and lowered self-esteem. Who wants to keep doing something that embarrasses them, or makes them look stupid in the eyes of their peer group?

2. With lackluster victories, we find that we spend disproportional amounts of time trying to motivate ourselves (or others) in an attempt to accomplish the things that do not inwardly and innately excite us anyway. Why? Because it does not play to our strengths in the first place.

3. Because we are not excited about what we are doing or with whom we are associating, we have to fake the feeding of our passion. We engage in ceremonial activities, events, and celebrations to force feed our appearance of being passionate.

4. This, in turn, is visible through an individual's lack of stepping up to an opportunity to assume ownership. Then we are left with abdication, excuses, procrastination, and people seemingly being oblivious to needs or situations.

Notice that most people live by warped logical mental blueprints or have mental DNA destined for the "suc" zone.

While working with Boeing as the single longest invited leadership consultant and performance speaker at the Boeing Leadership Center, and strategizing with their global Human Capital development leaders, while simultaneously working with Anheuser-Busch's leadership development team, it became clear that in-order to create ownership DNA within the new professionals they were adding to their teams, it started with ensuring that people were positioned for victories, and that systems and environments were created to support that endeavor!

You can see this concept play out with positive (and unfortunately, far too often negative) results, as you look at major businesses. Systems have matured that allow individuals with success and victories to their credit to ascend upwards into positions where they can finally, truly, screw up! This is not a commentary about them as people, as I am sure that, in most cases, these are good people who mean well. The reality is that they are placed into a position and expected to assume ownership, yet they lack the complete competency necessary to execute their roles as true performers. This is adversely impacted by their own vanity that precludes them from asking for help.

Owners sign the front of a check.
Losers own the experience of signing the back of checks, while blaming the name on the front for why they are poor!

This model holds true for both the blue-collar aspects of the organization and the white-collar side of the organization. Whether engaging professionals in the Centurion or Baby-Boomer Generations, or the younger, entry-level side of the X / Y / YouTube (Millennials) Generation.

There has to be a way to transition yourself and others away from "suc" and always towards success, wouldn't you think?

That would be a resounding YES, and here is how you do it! In order to create a universe where you and others assume OWNERSHIP of your positions in life and become victors instead of victims, there are six specific ways every successful person and organization go about doing it!

Need another example?

Some organizations engineer a culture of one-team, one-organization, and thus, one-success. Southwest Airlines posted 90 consecutive quarters of profitability at a time when practically all other airlines sustained continued deficit operations, bankruptcy management, and cut-back mentalities. How, you may ask, could Southwest do this? Simple. By instilling into every employee and team member, at every level, that if the organization is not the choice of consumers, they do not make money. If they do not make money, no one wins in the end. While most major legacy airlines boast turn around times of 45 to 60 minutes on jets, with between eight and twelve ramp professionals, Southwest can turn a jet in 13 to 30 minutes, with three professionals. Everyone at Southwest understands, when a jet is on the ground the team loses money. Therefore, everyone has a sense of urgency to assist in any way they can to ensure the jet is turned expeditiously!

This is a team which assumes ownership in multiple ways to ensure Performance Execution!

There is never a lack of people who are envious of others' accomplishments, but I have never seen a line of people who are envious of the work it took to generate those accomplishments – have you?

Performance Execution is attained by a very small percentage of any observed segmentation. Whether we defer to the athletic examples and statistics in the X-Factor chapter or the level of competency you maintain as diagnostically illustrated in the **Player Capability Index**® chapter, you determine the performance bubble within which you live.

Performance Execution is about individuals standing up, acting like, operating like, and being VIPs in everything they consciously do!

Appendix 1

Practical Application:
Working the Generational Diversity Gap will be Your Organizational
Asset to Performance Execution

CAUTION: When profiling groups or making generalizations about differing segmentations like generational groups, be mindful that there may be exceptions, and even differences within individual groups. There are limited exceptions to a rule, any rule, and thus, this rule as well.

Organizations which attain Performance Execution will face another performance factor. Consider Fundamental Commonality factor seven (beyond the original six presented in this book) as universal to successful organizations and individuals.

We have had decades of teeter-totter conditioning to not be racist or sexist, whether that is professionally or personally. In fact, if you explore Amazon.com or conduct a Google search on gender or ethnicity issues around management, leadership, interpersonal interactions, teams, work group dynamics, succession planning, developing high-po's, and general success, there are literally hundreds of authors, and thousands of informational options available. But the functioning reality is that generational understanding and acceptance really is the new variable which impacts performance and Performance Execution. Fewer than a dozen individuals internationally have penned more than five books or programs on generational diversity as an X-Factor success variable, and by 2008, the top-referenced authority on the topic, Ron Zemke, had already been deceased for two years.

So let's explore generational segmentation analysis among every successful person, organization, and enterprise today that affords them the unique ability to deliver Performance Execution!

Whether you are managing or selling to others, there are some explosive, parallel reasons why people are mentally, and even more often now, physically ejecting from your propositions. The person that grasps this reality in the future will have a remarkable performance advantage among their peer group and within their marketplace.

When you reflect upon the generational extremes, the answers may differ in how a person builds their X-Factor, and how they explore what constitutes a powerful Player Capability Index. Which USFx2x4 will have the ability to move and have meaning to one segmentation, while having little to no affect on another generational segmentation, and how you can go about pulling together individuals for alignment via the differing mission statements.

Recently, I started seeing the dots begin to connect when I was talking with an all-star manager for the Sonic restaurant chain about why he abruptly left for a competitor. I noticed the same thing when I spoke with the continuously successful senior pharmaceutical representative who resigned from Pfizer Pharmaceutical, only to immediately go to work for a direct competitor, and take with her significant market share. I noticed the same with the top Army National Guard recruiter in the nation who resigned / transferred from one state, and moved to another state to resume recruiting. The individual instantly begin setting new state records. Same with the mass migration of Generation Xers and Generation Yers from a city to a neighboring states metro market. So what are the reasons for these ejections?

In a survey of 1,000 individuals, (which is significantly more people than a typical Gallup Poll population index!) who were simultaneously surveyed by both Robert Half & Associates, (one of the nations largest employment personnel service firms) and Express Employment Professionals, (the second-largest employment services firm lead by Robert Funk, CEO, who for years has penned a content-rich how-to themed column for *Professional Performance Magazine (www.ThePerformanceMagazine.com)*, several commonalities were found to be true. The next time you attempt to engage another person, whether it is from a pure managerial / leadership / coaching perspective, or from the position of selling goods or services to another person, consider how you can forecast which of the following would be of most value to your intended audience, and therefore, how to best position your approach to ensure you address their value interest. People today are pulled into an engagement and are therefore, ejected based upon the following:

1. People want to feel appreciated and respected by others!

2. People want to feel what they do has meaning and that which they contribute to, or work on, has meaning!

3. People want to feel as if they bring value, are valued, and are seen as a valuable asset to their organizations and individual work units!

4. People want to participate in collaborations more today than in isolated situations or projects!

5. People want to have their immediate needs addressed and know how the activities around them can feed these most basic primal needs!

What became evident through every interview on ejecting, and from every survey benchmarked against what others do, is that people do not eject initially for any financial reasons (it costs too much, it does not pay enough, I did not get the expected bonus or raise, etc.). It is always the justifier after one of, or a series of the power five have been triggered.

The peak performer, whether as a leader among others or selling to others, has developed the keen ability to laser-focus a conversation or a needs-analysis on six core Q&A areas. By asking yourself or another party these six questions, you can find the blueprint for how best to engage the other person to determine why someone might eject from your approach, and thus, how to re-tool your approach to enlist them into your proposition. Consider the depth of value of each individual consultative Q&A and really ask: WHO, WHAT, WHEN, WHERE, WHY, and HOW?

These six simple questions can draw out from the other person what their true motivators are, and how best to package your approach to avoid mass ejection from your center of influence. To turbo-charge this approach, consider the power of positive gain you can attain today by tapping into the power of Generation Diversity. In other words, determine the power of the differences in today's five generational segmentations in the workplace, and what each can bring as a performance advantage.

Generational segmentation understanding is challenging today because it seems as if everyone has differing names for different segmentations. Let's create a template that will allow any future data to be used as an overlay for application. The United States Census Bureau places individuals from birth through death into five categories, so we are going to use these labels as our template:

1. Centurions – Those over 65
2. Baby Boomers – Those between the ages of 42 and 65
3. Generation X – Those between the ages of 32 and 42
4. Generation Y – Those between the ages of 22 and 32
5. Millennials – Those between the ages of 16 and 22

Recognizing that the likelihood of the government changing one of its models is very low, if we use this same segmentation template, we can have a constant by which to apply these generational Performance Execution ideas. Take what you know, and what we present here, along with information from any other experts you come across in the future, as a means to benchmark what you have on your present teeter-totter and who may need to be added to your teeter-totter in the future in order to influence success.

People enter the workplace environment between the ages of 17 and 21, and they begin retiring after the ages of 55 to 65. So our template for understanding our workforce and minimizing ejection situations would be: there are five distinct generational segmentations in our workplace today, each with similarities and distinct differences in operation.

As you read this template, I may be placing you into a segmentation that differs from what you would be labeled in a more macro-societal context. Just understand that the workplace reflects society, and there are always the most matures and extreme youth, so we will just use as an overlay the Census Bureau's model for our workplace perimeters:

1. Centurions (over 55): more structured, conservative, risk-adverse, dedicated, loyal, formal, willing to put in their time for rewards, organization-focused, patriotic, and autocratic in their decision flow.

2. Baby Boomers (38-55): more competitive, materialistic, accepting of situational change, title-driven, like systems, more democratic in their decision flow.

3. Generation X (28-38): more impulsive, entitlement-driven, more outside-focused, the transition population, more social, and look to the workplace as an extension of the social-peer network, more flexible, transition generation, more consensus in their decision flow.

4. Generation Y (21-28): more impatient, short attention spans and interests, more liberal, need immediate gratification, more collaboration-based, technologically savvy, influenced by social network(s), lower interpersonal skill set, more environmentally sensitive and focused, more open to change and multiple professional options as a way of life.

5. Generation Millennial (17-21): more open, embrace change, instant multi-stimulation, more socially connected to others, more independent, conservative, and dedicated to others, want people to just direct them to action because they feel overwhelmed by choices.

The five distinct age groups and generational segmentations of every organization are really tomorrow's performance differentiators. This is really tomorrow's true diversity imperative, as each segmentation actually brings value. Each segmentation can learn and benefit from one another. If you embrace these five groups and their unique traits, characteristics, values, beliefs, and attitudes, the height of success that can collectively be attained is limitless. Unfortunately, in most environments today, we set these five up for confrontational encounters, and time wastes away.

As you look around your community and organizations, you will notice that we have reached a point where performance improvement in many areas has reached a stalling point. The reason may be as simple as the high school science project with the simple pot of water and the frog. People have become too comfortable with their overall situation(s) in life, as if they were the frog in a pot of water with the heat slowly being turned up. Eventually that frog will die, and so, too, will many communities and organizations. The true performer has the ability to assess situations as if they were the frog being tossed into a pot of already boiling water. What would that frog (YOU) do in that situation?

Now do you have a more thorough grasp of why people today eject from you, your offer, and your organizations? Understanding ejection dynamics and how that will impact today's Generation Diversity will elevate your performance engagements for greater success!

The days of a wide-brush-stroke approach to engaging each individual in an organization, as if they were crafted from the same mold, are gone!

The ability to fluidly connect, understand, respect, (not necessarily agree or disagree!) and motivate the generational segmentations in a business organization will be the differentiator between greatness and existence. There is a direct and very defined connection between how your personal managerial-leadership style and age or generational segmentation affect your performance and your ability to execute action.

This is also true for the methods by which businesses today operate and how they may need to evolve to attain alignment of their Human Capital assets for the future.

Again, the five generational segmentations (as I initially outlined in my 2000 book COACHING for IMPACT: The Art & Leadership of Generational Coaching, Brown Books, ISBN# 0-9641240-3-3 / USA $29.95) can be identified most typically as operating from these motivators:

1. Centurions – The 55 and older segmentation tends to be more structured, more command-and-control driven and responsive, formal, exhibit traditional "American values," more regimented, reserved, focused, loyal, long-term oriented, purpose- and value-driven, willing to make sacrifices, organizationally committed.

2. Baby Boomers (and the Eco Boomers) – Those between 38 and 55 years of age tend to be less structured, more materialistic, like to be recognized and awarded for their achievements and contributions, change-resistant, more vocal and outgoing, very competitive, not as loyal because they have seen loyalty is not always a two-way street, contingent commitment, more loyal to an industry than a specific organization, title-driven, more formal education and learning styles.

3. Generation Xers – The 28 to 38 crowd tends to be more action-oriented, boundary-pushing, of the digital generation, interactive learning styles, opportunity-driven, trust more in themselves than in institutions and organizations, socialization and friend-oriented, entitlement-driven, accepting of change, more instant-gratification-oriented, more independent than generational segmentations before them, dislike rules and protocols.

4. Generation Yers – Those in the 21 to 28 segmentation have open minds but shorter attention spans, social network-driven, digitally-fluent operators, more globally versed, more sound-bite and cursory knowledge on lots of differing issues but limited depth of detail, like unlimited opportunities or

choices, need more diverse stimulation, do not like to be told what to do, lack depth of social etiquette, are driven by change, technologically savvy.

5. Millennials – The 17 to 21 individuals are looking for purpose and value opportunities. Change is normal, and they are relationship-driven, although very connected via the Internet world and not as savvy with actual interpersonal skills. Idealistic, technology-driven, highly socially conscious, short-term focused. This is a generation with a dichotomy, where a large percentage actually exhibit Centurion/Mature generational segmentation traits, while at the same time those of Generation Y.

To enhance your Performance Execution ability and connectedness with others, you should approach individuals from the perspective of how their generational segmentation likes to operate.

We become who we have always been…
Individuals typically operate outwardly from our inward generational
segmentations!"

By fluidly engaging individuals one-on-one or within group dynamics, you can attain a higher level of individual performance and group effectiveness. By evaluating how individual segmentation operates, leaders can take the mystery and angst out of trying to determine how best to engage and motivate their team. They can also reduce, if not eliminate, micro-management by merely delivering the minimal needs to each segmentation, and attaining maximum performance!

To maintain a real-time ability to remind yourself of the influences on differing generational segmentations' teeter-totters, here is a useful map I use when consulting with clients to assist individuals and leaders in gaining an operating understanding of others. We have experienced great success with this tool with teams ranging from the Army National Guard, Anheuser-Busch, El Paso Energy, and Harley-Davidson, to Boeing, NASA and Western CPE (the leading provider of CPE courses for CPAs in America). By using our ABC MAPS® model you can gain a better, and real-time understanding of the teeter-totter influences and operating DNA of each generational segmentation.

You can run the template in your mind as you engage others. You can take an organization of size and break individuals down into their respective generational segmentations, have each complete the following exercise, omitting their own generation, and then bring the group back together to debrief, and build an organizational master map of how each segmentation sees the others on the ABC MAPS model. It can become a powerful revelation.

These responses may radically influence or change an organization's operating teeter-totter and influence X-Factor attainment, by, (as Jim Collins in *Good to Great* would say) having the right people on your bus, and the right people in the right place for a change!

Here is how the model works (you can build an Excel spreadsheet of descriptions for macro understanding). Use each letter as a reference trigger to evaluate another generational segmentation objectively and identify the descriptors, words, or phrases which come to mind for each category.

It is through a better understanding of the uniqueness and similarities within each generational segmentation, that you can see the cultural challenges and alignment opportunities. It is through this same diagnostic understanding that you can begin to see paths for better integration and harmonious performance execution that feed each segmentations' needs. Remember, there are no right or wrong, good or bad answers – just observational responses.

ABC MAPS

Category	Generational Segmentation Descriptors
ATTRIBUTES	_____
BEHAVIORS	_____
CHARACTERISTICS	_____
MORALS	_____
ATTITUDES	_____
PERSONALITY	_____
SPIRITUALITY	_____

The more that groups understand the diversity of influences on another person's teeter-totter, the more a whole new level of Performance Execution can be attained. This model can radically alter how you engage others, communicate and delegate among your peers and contemporaries, attract others to your cause, and even impacts the retention initiatives of organizations domestically and internationally.

A twenty-four month survey of the top CEOs and HR leaders from the top 100 largest CPA firms in America, along with more than 500 business executives from small to Fortune 100 businesses, led to a mega list of differing ideas on how to attract or retain differing generational segmentations in the workplace today. Consider some of these ideas, and consider which generational segmentations they would have the greatest association with:

ATTRACTING	RETAINING
1. Pay & benefits	1. Practice what you preach
2. Work life balance	2. Compensation packages
3. Show opportunities	3. Frequent evaluations
4. Reputation	4. Paid time off
5. Flexibility	5. Communicate upwards
6. Team environment	6. Appreciation
7. Signing bonus	7. Advancement opportunity
8. Referral bonus / bounty	8. Personal investments
9. Incentive compensation plans	9. Firm activities
10. Recruiters	10. I.T. systems
11. Search firms	11. Shopping days
12. Attractive work space	12. Paid ski vacations
13. Technology	13. Timeshare vacations

14. Industry trade show booths / sponsorships

14. Company car / car allowance

15. Open houses

15. Contests

16. Career fairs

16. Tenure gifts

17. College fairs

17. Management reputation

18. College department fairs

18. Performance-specific bonus

19. Website ads on your home page

19. Trust

20. Banner ads on others websites

20. Training

21. Monster.com /CareerBuilder. com

21. Educational reimbursement

22. Internships / co-ops

22. Fun work environment

23. Alternate work hour options

23. Pay for CPE

24. Job rotation

24. Pay association dues

25. Pen articles

25. Pay for self-study

26. Be a regular media guest

26. Provide in-house CPE

27. TYPros & Chamber

27. Health club fees paid

28. Partner strategically in community

28. Gift cards

29. Overseas recruitment

29. Top managers cook for team

30. Give scholarships

30. Team trips

31. Give post scholarships

31. Day outings

32. Do speaking engagements

32. Breakfast meetings

33. Recruitment teams (by age segment)	33. Casual dress
34. Hire away award winners from others	34. Strengthen existing teams
35. ID laid-off workers from downsized firms	35. Provide better offices
36. Create an Info bureau	36. Provide pick of office furnishings
37. Contact local government career centers	37. Happy hours
38. Community event participation	38. Community event participation
39. Sports & entertainment tickets	39. Sports & entertainment tickets
40. Volunteer for civic / community events	40. Stress outing (take team to driving range or engage in other stress projects, so they can "let it out"...)
41. College case study competitions	41. Donate vacation time / PR
42. Host round-table Q&A about organization	42. Offer retirement slot to retain needed older professionals
43. Go after retirees	43. Have annual holiday shopping sprees
44. Go back to retired all-stars	44. Virtual office opportunity
45. Have annual service pins	45. Involve spouses and families in organization events and celebrations
46. Fun environment	46. Work life balance
47. Comprehensive innovative benefits	

Understanding generational segmentation diversity and similarities will be the next wave of organizational success dynamics. The ability to blend, assimilate, align resources, and ensure that everyone is truly in their X-Factor, is the essence of Performance Execution.

This evolution and change in how training endeavors are designed and launched will be adversely affected by this diversity. How individuals are engaged, managed, motivated, etc. will all be impacted by this diversity.

It is not a matter of right versus wrong, nor good versus bad. It is the new Performance Execution reality. Generational diversity exists. We have created it, and let it out of the box, and there is no getting it back in and closed. By recognizing the reality of what the teeter-totter influencers may be for each individual generational segmentation, what their X-Factors may actually be, and how each goes about assuming ownership or abdicating it, you will be able to attain greater levels of Performance Execution.

The more efficient you become in recognizing the generational segmentation application upon IQ + EQ, the faster you will attain competitive PQ output.

The percentage of "suc" situations should decline, individuals can be addressed head on, and success can now be attained at simultaneous levels both within our interactions with others, and within our organizations!

Appendix 2

Practical Application:
Awakening the Leadership Potentials Within You and Others...

Putting Performance Execution to Work With the "Control" and "Entrepreneurial" Forces within You and Your Organization for Risk Management Success *(cForce™ v. eForce™)*

eForce™ = Entrepreneurial Forces
cForce™ = Control Forces

Want to gain a better understanding of why the Savings and Loan (S&L) implosion happened in the 1980s, the Dot Com implosion happened in the 1990s, or the sub-prime home loan and Wall Street implosion happened in the 2000s? It really is very simple: just grasp, understand, and apply the cForce™ versus eForce™ concepts and their horrifying implications upon Performance Execution, and you will have a clear, undisputed answer to Performance Execution and VIP behavior, or performance implosion and sustained VUP behavior!

Then, as an overlay, apply the Six Fundamental Commonalities of Performance Execution to the eForce and cForce models, and these implosions become very obvious – WOW!

In late 2008, the world found itself in what the media and unsophisticated political leaders labeled an "economic crisis." By combining the performance information in this book, with the eForce and cForce models, it becomes obvious what was really being experienced was not an economic crisis, but actually an economic realignment to reality!"

Great leaders do not have answers at the outset of any situation. What they do have is the innate ability or the trained skill to ask the right questions at the right time of the right people, and then, answers always reveal themselves!

To attain Performance Execution success within any organization, you must engage the traditional decision-makers (eForce and cForce players) and understand the historical teeter-totter of these individuals, while simultaneously engaging Four Core Stakeholders (financial, technical, users, advocates – this concept will be explained in greater detail shortly) as allies!

"The task of the leader is to get his (her) people from where they are to where they have not been."
-Henry Kissinger

Leland Harty, CPA and former strategic executive with GE Capital, (and a colleague of mine) and I were exploring real-time Performance Execution case studies in our own business circles. What dawned on us is a whole new model for looking at:

1. The decisions we must make to attain Performance Execution

2. The actual individual tasked with making said decisions for Performance Execution

Things are changing. In a simpler time, traditional decision-making and Performance Execution within an organization, as well as how individuals addressed the levels of risk, and even contained risk, was very exact and predictable.

Historically, organizations would follow preset guidelines to reach the wisest decision. They adhered to strictly-defined procedures, protocols, roles of responsibility, and accountability. Individuals, divisions, departments, business units, institutions, agencies, and even regulatory entities have long since been conditioned to serve precisely-defined roles – serve as a Control Force (cForce) in the execution process.

Examine a traditional business school diagram. Consider all of the essential functional positions you would need for a successful organization, an ideal organization, a lean organization. You would recognize that every position within that diagram falls into one of two distinct groups.

Each of these historical entities of a business organizational chart is either:

1. **eForces** – "**Entrepreneurial Forces**" were charged with being cutting-edge, creative, marketers, sellers, account builders, and acquirers of increased market share. These people were more risk-players and risk-takers and they were rewarded accordingly. Traditionally, these players would be labeled on an organizational diagram as: CEO, Leaders, R&D, Sales, Marketing, Public Relations, Customer Service, Advocates, Emerging Market Builders, etc. Their compensation structure was tied to performance, and the greater they performed, the greater the earning possibilities.

2. **cForces** – "**Control Forces**" were fixated as the rule enforcers, regulators, auditors, actuaries, accountants, and watchdogs of activities. Traditionally, these players would be labeled within an organizational diagram as: CFO, COO, Controller, Legal, Audit, Accounting, Regulatory, Administration, and Managers. Outside of an organization, the cForces would be: the Board, regulators, auditing companies, industry policing associations, elected government leaders (Congressmen, Presidents), shareholders, and even the media.

These internal players within an organization were expected to be more in control and introverted in their performance; their compensation was predetermined and typically limited.

These two traditional roles would battle over decisions. Each eForce and cForce player was very predictable in their actions. It was the never-ending game of push and pull between these forces that drove organizational decision-making, growth, expansion, regulation, and maintenance of business transactions!

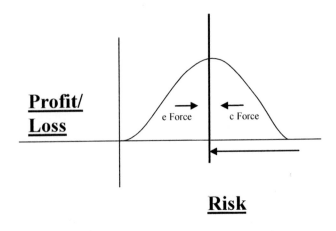

Performance Execution

Both eForce and cForce segments could possess VIPs, and X-Factor performance would be demonstrated by both sides.

It was the power of the players, within either the cForce or eForce category, that typically drove a decision, as well as how it would be viewed, either as risk tolerance or risk aversion.

Traditionally, this would also dictate where that Critical Divide™ point would be, and at what point a decision could be expected or predicted. This point is the Operating Risk Level™ (ORL™). It allows both leaders engaged in decision-making to determine if it is acceptable, and if each historical cForce™ and eForce™ operative is performing as historically expected.

Managing the potential "veto" powers in the decision-making process was, and is, critical for sound decision-making and risk management control. Traditionally, it would be expected that equal input (50/50) would be sought before making a decision. It was also expected, and typically delivered, that individuals would stay within their realm of standard operating procedure (cForce and eForce people acted like cForce and eForce people).

Historically, organizations avoided many of the extraordinary decisions being made today, decisions that subsequently can be seen as having direct linkage to future organizational trauma. In many sad instances between 2000 and 2009, the world business stage saw implosion after implosion. Most of these implosions occurred because traditional cForce and eForce players did not execute their jobs from the category to which they were tasked, but were instead expected by the Board, CEO and consumers to operate outwardly!

To better understand the great constraints that these two sets of decision-makers assume, consider that any individual decision that is made by a cForce or eForce player is comprised of four intrinsic sub-decision phases.

Within the realm of the eForce and cForce™ players, there are four core functions to a sound decision. These functions were traditionally assigned to the appropriate players. Many times, oversight by one or all of these four potential "veto" stakeholders caused the increased risk associated with the decision-making process!

Whether you are engaged in critical self-thought or interacting with others, there are four sub-decisions to every overall decision. These four sub-decisions are especially noticeable when you make decisions in environments or situations perceived to have an element of risk associated with them.

The four sub-decisions are each made by critical stakeholders in the decision-making process, and each stakeholder is responsible for implementation of risk management protocols. Therefore, the Four Core Stakeholders™ (for any decision) that must be rallied and converted into advocates and/or allies are:

1. **Financial stakeholders**, who scrutinize the decision from the financial perspective. They are traditionally cForce players and are compensated in a very structured and limited manner.

2. **Technical stakeholders**, who scrutinize the decision from the technical perspective, to determine what the decision will or will not deliver. They are traditionally cForce players and compensated in a very structured and limited manner.

3. **Users or implementer stakeholders**, who will implement the decision, and are typically concerned with how they will embrace, respond, or react to a decision. They base it upon their perceived level of risk associated with adhering to or avoiding the decision. They are traditionally eForce™ players and compensated in a more performance-based, production-oriented manner with high yield capability.

4. **Advocate/Champion/Coach stakeholders**, (or your internal voice, at times) who do not have a direct influence on a decision, but can brief you on how to engage the other stakeholders to gain allies. Traditionally eForce, this may be your internal voice that pushes you to buy something on impulse, only later to be followed by buyer's remorse when you reflect upon it from the vantage point of one of the other three stakeholders' perspectives!

Engaging the Four Core Stakeholders as allies simply involves the identification and engagement of each sub-decision!

There are additional factors influencing which force toward which an individual might evolve. The factors we have previously discussed that make-up an individual's or organization's operational teeter-totter may include: age, gender, culture, race, educational background, and previous experiences. People traditionally followed very defined migration patterns in their work selection, which, when combined with their decision-making style, can create the basis for their risk tolerance or risk aversion.

Organizations used to be structured in such a manner that the methodology behind the division of labor created a very defined role for decision-making.

These roles were further reinforced by individual personality styles and the personality style of a division, business unit, department, or regulatory entity.

Traditionally, these forces were aligned to ensure that organizations had committed the highest level of integrity to decision-making. Individuals' social or personality styles were tied to these force categories as well. It was a sure bet that the analytical and amiable personalities would most often evolve towards the cForce positions, while the driver, Type A, and expressive personalities would typically be the eForce players.

Keeping both the historical eForces and the cForces in alignment was the responsibility of:

1. The Board of Directors, with appropriately-assigned individual board members assuming authority, auditing, command, and control capacities for each core operational / functional area.

   This is critical for organizational Performance Execution success, as every key executive should have a board member to validate or serve as an accountability partner!

2. The outside regulatory entities that the board and organization employ to keep the board, and by default the organization, in-check. An example of this is a legitimate auditing firm, which also understands the eForce and cForce methodology!

3. From here, responsibility moves upwards and outwards to government regulatory entities, Congress, and the President.

4. Ultimately, it proceeds to the shareholders, voters, and the media as further watchdog operatives!

So what has happened to kill Performance Execution? Engaging the new decision-makers as eForce and cForce players should be done with an understanding of whether the people we expect to make these decisions are playing from their X-Factor and truly possess the Player Capability Index credentials to be doing so.

Change your attitude, change your destination.

Reality check: Traditional decision-making has imploded in the workplace. The disasters of corporate America and around the globe speak for themselves once you understand the truths detailed with Performance Execution!

Lines of accountability used to be very clearly defined. However, responsibilities within an organization are no longer exact and predictable.

Expectations. Checks and balances. Previously such items were clearly described in an organizational diagram of positions and personalities. Today, however, they are no longer exact or predictable.

Things are changing. The way functional entities and individuals within an organization are compensated has changed. Individuals want to be compensated for performance through methods that are outside the norms of traditional organizations, which is not the way in which they were initially constructed to grow and expand. It is no longer based upon very clear, and in many cases, capped compensation opportunities.

Within organizations, wise decision-making has become a lost science, and a state of chaos has ensued. With many individuals, divisions, departments, business units, institutions, agencies, and even regulatory entities (including new-line Democratic and Republican ORL and cForce and eForce personas) occupying an organizational diagram position of cForce or eForce, yet conducting themselves as the opposite persona, it has all but obliterated the check-and-balance system upon which the organization was predicated.

This has significantly impacted an organization's real ORL, not the organizational-diagram-implied ORL, that is based upon the expected cForce and/or eForce operatives' conduct and functionality.

eForces were once defined as "entrepreneurial" in nature and charged with being cutting-edge, creative, marketers, sellers, account builders and acquirers. Because these people more often are risk-players, they are rewarded accordingly in today's business economy. This is even encouraged and is visible as these individuals take even greater risks without regard for ramifications – the rewards always outweigh the losses. If one of them does wreak complete havoc upon others, he or she will still arise from the storm a wealthy individual – greed has motivated the player!

Some of the leading graduate schools today teach curriculum centering on the price you must be willing to pay to succeed. Witness the Ivan Boskeys and Michael Millikens of the world from the 1980s, who stole billions, only to be fined millions. Perhaps this is what grew the Fastows (ENRON), Kozlowskis (TYCO), the Wall Street Executives, mortgage industry players, and Congressmen/Women and others of the 1990s, which exploded in the 2000s!

When you glamorize the deal at any cost, you should not be surprised with hidden costs of the scam!

cForces were once defined as the rule-enforcers, regulators, auditors, actuaries, accountants, and watchdogs of activities. Once paid in limited capacity with limited upward movement in income, these cForce individuals challenged the premise of the organizational diagram upon which all functionality of an organization is predicated, and were rewarded for net profitability. This has created a whole new attitude, culture, and teeter-totter, which has affected phantom X-Factors: expectation of entitlement and DNA within environments to become competitive with the eForce players.

Compounding this trauma is that, if the internal entities traditionally tasked with cForce roles assume an eForce mentality and behavior, then it is incumbent upon leaders to ensure that the external forces employed to ensure stability are cForces. When outside entities bastardize the cForce responsibility and become eForce players as well, it is only a matter of time before that entity and its players implode and cease to exist!

CASE STUDY Commentary: The ENRON Corp. (Houston, TX) and Arthur Andersen (NYC, NY) implosions happened because they should have happened!

Every position traditionally diagrammed to be a cForce morphed into an eForce. No one recognized this, nor initiated any steps to safeguard against the bastardization of the organization. When the CEO assumed an eForce operational style, he assumed his CFO, COO, and audit, finance, and

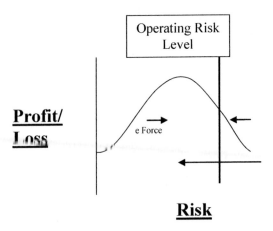

**Profit/
Loss**

Risk

accounting departments, would assume their fiduciary responsibilities as cForce players. Surely, if they morphed into eForce personas, outside cForces (the Board, the audit company, regulators, associations, Congressional Committees entrusted by the citizens to watch out for them) would not waiver, but remain steadfast as a check-and-balance to prevent anyone on the team from switching roles.

If not for these people, surely the President of the United States (as a cForce player) would hold everyone accountable. Even then, if all of these cForce functioning positions were assumed by eForce personas, surely the legions of employees internal to an organization would assume their appropriate cForce roles.

This situation alone is perhaps a more accurate explanation as to why so many companies, non-profits, and government entities in the 2000s imploded. Everyone assumed an entitlement mentality and an eForce persona of "hooray for me and to hell with everyone else!"

Witness that most all employees at ENRON were overpaid and both the Republican and Democratic parties and their elected officials were given donations at near parity with one another. Businesses like these will never be fully prosecuted, as it would be very politically incorrect to indict and send to jail the thousands of employees who deserve it, based upon their repeated and long-term behaviors – or were the cForces just acting like eForces with no counter balance?

Either way, the end result is, the critical divide fades away, and no one sees or measures any level of RISK!

What once served as a safety measure to organizational decision-making, and provided a level of assurance that there would be some level of sound decision-making taking place (balanced teeter-totter resulting in a sound X-Factor being exhibited) in the face of risk, has all but disappeared.

Managing the potential "veto" powers in the decision-making process has faded. With a blurring of the cForce and eForce lines of accountability, everyone wants greater financial rewards and performs to that standard. The STOP Model is nowhere to be seen, alignment among the interrelated five mission statements does not exist, and individuals whose Player Capability Index would indicate "empty," are making critical decisions that affect others' futures!

So the four sub-decisions that were, and still are, made on a daily basis, (and that do still influence risk levels, profitability levels, and loss levels) have become overpowered by eForce players. Imagine what happens within your organization if the following four risk management decision roles are facilitated by eForce mindsets:

1. Financial stakeholders no longer scrutinize the decision from the financial perspective.

2. Technical stakeholders no longer scrutinize the decision from the technical perspective.

3. User and implementer stakeholders will no longer be concerned about how they will embrace, respond, or react to a decision.

4. Advocate/Champion/Coach stakeholders will no longer brief you on how best to engage the other stakeholders to gain allies.

If each of these people becomes an eForce player, they will expect to be compensated in a more performance-based, production-oriented manner, and all appropriate risk management controls will disappear!

Organizations do a disservice to their ORL™ and impede their Performance Execution ability to make wise decisions and manage risk effectively when they abdicate the cForce function within their organization and surround themselves with entities, players, institutions, departments, Board members, consultants, governmental entities, and officials which assume an eForce mentality and compensation expectation standard!

In today's workplace, the reality of the traditionally-aligned eForce and cForce functional lines and positions are disappearing at a rapid speed. Recognize how the blending of these traditionall-aligned positions can impact wise organizational decision-making and reduce negatives associated with poor risk-taking judgment.

Imagine where the United States and world economies might be if colossal implosions (such as those of Countrywide, Fannie Mae, Freddie Mac, AIG, Merrill Lynch, Lehman Brothers, ENRON, Global Crossing, WorldCom, Arthur Andersen, and others) would not have occurred, due to players having held true to their lines of accountability, integrity, and ethics, and ensured that both eForce and cForce players worked within the critical divide equation.

More importantly, notice how the eForces and cForces of the traditional organizational structure and the new organizational structure create a bell curve energy force.

Notice how that builds to the point of a critical divide, and how that can influence wise organizational decision-making in uncertain times.

Organizations today have evolved silently overnight into a dangerous architecture of who now serves in the cForce and eForce roles. What was traditionally structured to provide organizational balance in decision-making may now serve wildly with no checks and balances. Traditional cForce individuals now want to be rewarded as if they were eForce players, and cForce entities have assumed eForce behaviors to capitalize on greater financial gains without regard to long-term ramifications of their short-term decisions.

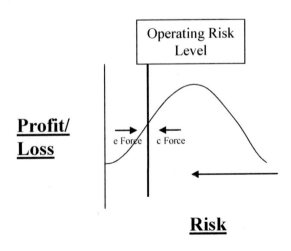

Traditional cForce roles within an organization that would have been introvert jobs or occupied by introverted individuals, and conversely, eForce roles or extrovert jobs and individuals are now being staffed with the opposite. Imagine an auditor or accountant that is a Type A, driver personality or a wildly social, expressive extrovert, and how this skews your decision matrix expectations.

Not everyone can be a celebrity, not everyone can be financially independent and wealthy, and not everyone is above being held accountable to earn VIP status and being told when they are just a VUP!

The opportunity for implosion by the blending of cForce and eForce players is compounded when the following groups abdicate their functionality, act complacent, or – even worse – all become eForce operatives, when a blend of the two is what is necessary!

1. Boards of Directors with appropriately-assigned individual board members assuming authority, auditing, command, and control capacities of each core operational / functional area of an organization.

2. Then outside regulatory entities that the board and organization employ to keep the board, and by default the organization, in check. An example of this is a legitimate auditing firm, which also understands the eForce and cForce methodology!

3. From here, the responsibility moves upward and outward to government regulatory entities, Congress, and the President.

4. Ultimately, it proceeds to the shareholders, voters, and the media as further watchdog operatives!

The critical divide can be adversely pushed too far the other way as well. A natural reaction (emotion-based) when the eForce has become too powerful and trauma has been inflicted, is to push too far in a cForce direction. This, too, can create trauma.

What needs to be done is to reflect upon the decisions that need to be made. If it is an eForce decision, or if it is a cForce decision, keep that in mind first. Then ask yourself who the person in that decision-making position is and whether they are an eForce or a cForce person. Let those answers guide how you go about getting 50/50 percent input from both forces.

Managing Performance Execution within ourselves, and among others, demands a balance of cForce players and eForce players. If an individual assumes a persona of the opposite force, it can only be accepted if certain provisions are made. It must be acknowledged, and individuals and systems must be in place from the beginning to hold each person accountable. Accountability must further be provided at every decision point throughout the planning and implementation process. This will allow for a critical divide which is more often balanced and objective - not out of balance, due to a tendency to overweigh a decision based upon only one force!

The more you understand about the people making eForce and cForce decisions, the more it will tell you about their teeter-totter, and where they are going. This includes understanding things such as what their true X-Factor is, what comprises their Player Capability Index, whether their mission statement is in alignment with the organization's, and if they have the USFx2x4 to deliver the performance results needed.

Are you dealing with windshield (transformers) or rearview mirror (terrorists) people? And who are you?

Always remember two questions that cForce and eForce dynamics guide you on: First, what type of decision needs to be made (c or e)? Second, what is the personality of the decision-maker (c or e)? This will allow you to forecast the types of decisions to be made!

Appendix 3

Practical Application:
Building Respectful Interactive RELATIONSHIPS with Others...

The Four Core Building Blocks to Performance Execution with
Another Person

Motivating relationships for Performance Execution at the micro need level and macro sustained mission statement level can be attained through a better understanding of who is on another person's teeter-totter, and what their real X-Factors are.

What does it really take to make a relationship with another person work? What does it take to cultivate and maintain healthy relationships with those with whom you work? How do you achieve sustained commitment and motivation by all parties?

The reverse may be easier to answer. Performance Execution with others will arise from your ability to ensure that you know what the valuable deposits are for the other person in forging a better, interactive relationship. To grasp this Performance Execution enhancement, let's explore the Relationship Cube®.

Remember the adage, "A picture is worth a thousand _____." I have noticed that every peak-performing Performance Execution VIP, either innately recognizes, or has been trained to recognize, that there are specific acts that serve as deposits into their relationships, which ultimately forge better relationships. For each person, (think generational diversity for teeter-totter variances in deposits) the deposits will be significantly different.

Consider motivated relationships in a work environment as an imaginary Relationship Cube. Each side is critical to holding a healthy relationship together. Visualize a cube with four sides labeled:

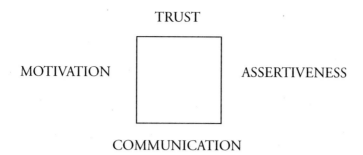

TRUST

MOTIVATION   ASSERTIVENESS

COMMUNICATION

The acts (or behavioral deposits) which allow each side of the Relationship Cube to stand solid are the answers to effective Performance Execution with other people.

There are four sides to the Relationship Cube model. Each side distinctly impacts relationships very quickly. The deposits under each, or within each, will either aid in maturing relationships and motivation, or, if they are challenged, neglected, or taken away, will cause them to implode. Let's explore each of these sides and what they mean.

1. TRUST – This is the top of every relationship between individuals and organizations. The more you know about another person's valued deposits for this specific category, (or side) the greater your ability to engage them for Performance Execution at any level.

Consider the typical deposits you could behaviorally deliver to create, foster, or promote, (in a healthy way) this side to exist: honesty, supportiveness, keeping your word, supporting others, maintaining confidence, integrity, etc. People today are born with innate "BS" meters and can detect untruths and deception. No one ever forgets betrayal!

The Performance Execution VIP understands that what may be a deposit on their Relationship Cube matrix may not be a deposit on another person's cube. Understanding what their deposits are, and subsequently making those deposits, strengthens your relationships with others so you can attain greater performance success.

2. ASSERTIVENESS – Allowing the other person to be proactive is essential for people to have a sense of meaning and feel comfortable in exhibiting their X-Factor.

Consider the deposits here as well. When you allow others to share their opinions, (as long as they are even remotely close to the issues at hand) you create more assertive behaviors. Shutting down people's opinions can be damaging. It can be a surefire way to kill off behaviors which are an asset to a healthy work place. By empowering others, assigning tasks according to people's X-Factor, acknowledging others, giving them freedom, and rewarding VIP performance, you breed more assertiveness outwardly from others, and inwardly from yourself.

3. MOTIVATION – Known as the fuel that drives people, when you feel or someone else feels robbed, you become unmotivated, and Performance Execution is exceedingly difficult at that moment in time.

Dispensing a genuine, sincere "Thank You" to those on your team is the fastest form of human motivation. Know what excites others and make those deposits accordingly. Whether it is increasing compensation, awards, rewards, recognition, empowerment, freedom, etc.!

4. COMMUNICATION – To many, this is seen as the foundation to any and every healthy and sustained relationship. People will sense whether you are being open, fair and consistent in your pursuit of clear communication.

Listen actively to others, ask appropriate and targeted questions, take notes, and associate and internalize the message (from your teeter-totter perspective) for greater understanding when engaging others!

Cultivating motivated relationships with others is essential for Performance Execution. Many times, this is an implosion point among dysfunctional groups, however, it is absolutely imperative for sustained success and efficiency within an organization. Healthy, motivated relationships cannot be neglected. Such apathy can be terminal. It is an invitation for a variety of downfalls. The organization can experience attrition, and peak performers may defect to the competition. Even worse, members of the organization may leave, and start a competing entity. This splits the overall business pie down to even smaller proportions!

Marcus Buckingham, a global practice leader formerly with the Gallup Organization, was paid to study, research, and offer some insight into these matters. Over the past decade, he has surveyed more than 2.5 million employees. He sought to discover key determinates to explain an employee's level of engagement in an organization, and what causes that Performance Execution involvement. Remember, earlier we discussed the 2008-2009 research about 71 percent of workers not being engaged in the workplace.

From the survey questions, three critical factors surfaced from the employee's perspective:

1. Do I know what is expected of me at work?
2. Do I have an opportunity to do what I do best every day?
3. Does my supervisor or someone at work care about me?

A leader's ability to foster and promote healthy relations with individuals and groups in the workplace will feed constructive responses to these three questions. In fact, with the existence of a solid Relationship Cube, individuals will become engaged in an organization. Then passion, motivation, and commitment will surface to comprise a thoroughly motivated group–that feeds the Ownership Model presented in Chapter Zero!

Imagine the level of immediate Performance Execution effectiveness you could experience if, in one of the first interactions you had with others, you asked what the deposits were for that person, for each of the four sides of the Relationship Cube. Imagine if, when a new person comes to your organization, you shared your list of deposits with them and asked for their list of operational deposits – WOW!

What typically causes people to become passive-aggressive and derail another person's performance, or miss cues on deposits? What causes you to become an organizational terrorist (and not a transformer) is a perception that people are making far more withdrawals in their interaction or relationship than making deposits.

Building healthy relationships with others is critical to your future Performance Execution success, whether it be with simple one-on-one interactions, or in forging collaborations and partnerships with groups. It is important, whether done in the social network universe where you may not actually see or know the other person, or with people you have interacted with for a long period of time. Think of the relationship cube as a bank account with the other person's name in/on it, and deposits into the Relationship Cube as currency. Would you know what the exchange rate would be with others? Do you know what acts of deposits are valued by the other party?

Psychology teaches us that men see money and currency as a power and control issue, while women see money and currency as a safety, security, and future needs issue. With most men, if you observe their performance, you will recognize that men dispose instantly of any currency involving coins, whereas women pocket and save coins. Watch men ordering at a Starbucks. Most will immediately dispose of their coin change into the TIPS jar at the counter, whereas more often then not, women will keep that change and retain it. Then, imagine that you ask a woman what they value. Like the example above, most of the time they will assign a value to every deposit into their Relationship Cube worth a penny, nickel, dime, quarter, half dollar, or perhaps even dollar. Men, on the other hand, usually do not see these deposits as actual deposits, much less worthy of a particular dollar value. You can see very quickly how we may inadvertently violate each other's Relationship Cube deposits, and thus implode success.

Performance Execution, and sensitivity to your EQ come from an understanding that you can NEVER attain Performance Execution from someone who feels as if they are interacting with others from an overdrawn perspective!

Appendix 4

Practical Application:
What Do You Do to Not "SUC" Right Now?

Putting Performance Execution Technologies to Work in Your Life as a Matter of Routine

L et's explore how to ensure that you continue along the path of Performance Execution, and identify tools you can utilize with yourself, as well as with others. Here are some practical homework assignments to test whether you really do "suc," or live for success.

Listen to the voices (your mental teeter-totter) in your head (as they apply to the alignment factors of the integrated mission statements) as you review and put into action (X-Factor attainment) each of these (Player Capability Index enhancers) Practical Application Tool Kit Activities (each drawing upon differing USFx2x4 variables).

50+ Practical Application Tool Kit Activities for Performance Execution Success

Practical Application Tool Kit Activities
Chapter Zero: Stand Up, Shut Up & Take Ownership

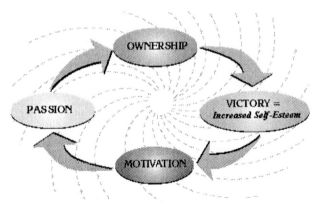

1. Starting with VICTORY, identify a personal mega accomplishment or victory that you have experienced in recent times. With that reference point, replay in your head that experience. How you felt, how it energized or re-MOTIVATED you, what it did for your PASSION. In turn, what did that do to cause you to assume more or less ownership of the endeavor that started the cycle?

2. Take the time management system that you use (PDA, Outlook, PALM, Blackberry, DayTimer, etc.) and log an action item or task at least one day each week for the next two months. Only enter an item that you know plays to your strongest ability and that you know would be an instant VICTORY for you. With that action task or item logged in your system, make sure you have that VICTORY each week, and chronicle that experience.

3. Inventory the last few awards, accolades, and citations you received for true VICTORY attainment. From these, recognize if those VICTORIES brought you satisfaction and MOTIVATED you. If, in fact, they drove your PASSION and caused you to assume greater control, responsibility, or OWNERSHIP of the endeavor (or person), let those VICTORIES serve as the reference points to what your X-Factor may be, and then apply these Performance Execution technologies to it for even greater success and VIP stature!

4. Practical Application – Identify an accountability plan of action you can design, and make a commitment to implement this chapter and bring Performance Execution to life for yourself.

_____

_____

_____

_____

_____

_____

_____

_____

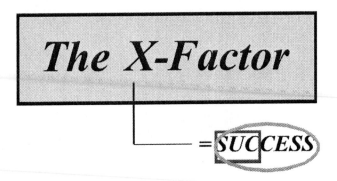

1. Make a NOT TO-DO list of at least five personal and five professional tasks for which you would normally volunteer or undertake, even though you know they play to your "suc-factor." Consciously work to not do them for the next ten days. Each time you catch yourself starting to do them, stop and make a note. See how many times you can catch yourself and direct your energy towards your true X-Factor(s).

2. Identify one major X-Factor that you possess, which most people do not realize you have, and actively seek opportunities to showcase that side of yourself for the next ten days to as many people and organizations as you can.

3. Get your Performance Review Assessment form for your professional position from your supervisor, HR Specialist, or personnel file. Benchmark it against any similar assessment instruments that your trade association may have for your kind of industry, business, and/or position. Make a composite instrument from the best-of-the-best tracking items to attain greater X-Factor performance. Now make a bi-weekly commitment to have your peers, boss, key customers, and yourself, conduct a thorough assessment of you. Track this data twice monthly for the next three months and see how your Performance Execution levels change, grow, improve, or falter.

4. Go to *www.JeffreyMagee.com* and send me an e-mail asking for a FREE copy of the "**Performance Execution Personnel Assessment Instrument.**" I have crafted this as a super assessment based upon the benchmarks of the top 38 Fortune 500 firms' personnel assessment instruments. I have also included input from many of today's top Performance Execution superstars.

Consider it a Performance Execution template, and adjust the limited line items you would need to change to make it most relevant for you.

5. Practical Application – Identify a second Performance Execution accountability plan of action that you can design and commit to implementing, that will bring this chapter to life for yourself. _____

_____

_____

_____

_____

_____

_____

_____

_____

_____

_____

$$C = (T2+A+P+E+C)E2xR = R$$

1. Sit down and craft a current RESUMÉ as if you were looking to hire yourself. What would be the most impressive action items you could promote about yourself? Use the individual letters of the index above to guide your resume building, keeping in mind that you should try to list the top ten most impressive items you can list for each letter.

2. If there is a way to identify a superstar in your organization, industry, or the industry in which you aspire to be, run this index on that entity to see what their X-Factor consists of. From this insight you can benchmark where you are in comparison, and what your next action plans must be for Performance Execution success.

3. Make a personal commitment that you will actively participate in one meaningful function or endeavor each month that enriches, grows, or adds new value to each individual variable of the formula. Sign up now for an educational or skill-based training class; subscribe to content-rich publications like *Professional Performance Magazine (www.ThePerformanceMagazine.com)*; read one non-fiction book per month; download podcasts, Internet radio programs, web-based courses, or online developmental shows such as www.HumanCapitalNetwork.TV; join networking groups which truly develop and inspire; etc.

4. Go to *www.jeffreymagee.com* for access to a full year of explosive, content-rich personal developmental articles for your personal and professional utilization. You can also share these with your organization and your personal e-mail address book!

5. Practical Application – Identify a third Performance Execution accountability plan of action that you can design and commit to implementing, that will bring this chapter to life for yourself.

_____

_____

_____

_____

Practical Application Tool Kit Activities
Chapter Three: Truth Three - USFx2x4® Is Your Only Differentiator

1. Go to *www.ThePerformanceMagazine.com* and start reading the different performance articles on marketing, branding, customer service, and selling. These articles have been penned by many of the world's leading Performance Execution stars. Download, save, and share them with others!

2. Take the RESUMÉ you prepared for Chapter Two, number one, (above) and benchmark it with those around you, those with whom you compete, and those who are ahead of you on the performance trail of life. Evaluate which variables you have that differ from theirs – better, faster, different, cost-effective.

3. Write down ten things you use every day in the course of your daily routine. Now evaluate what the predecessors to these ten items were in the marketplace to see how they were forward innovated (better, faster, different, and cost-effective) to warrant their existence. Let's use this drill to serve as a means to get your creative DNA going as you look into the mirror of life and evaluate who you are and what you could be.

4. Practical Application – Identify a fourth Performance Execution accountability plan of action that you can design and commit to implementing, which will bring this chapter to life for you.

_____

_____

_____

_____

_____

_____

_____

_____

_____

_____

_____

1. Whether you work for an organization or lead one, here is a pop quiz. Grab your business card right now and on the reverse side write down your organization's mission statement. Can you? If not, then how do you know if you are aligned with it?

2. To avoid falling out of your X-Factor, or tasking others outside of their X-Factor, place that card in your wallet as a reminder of about what you are supposed to be!

3. You should have each of the 5 Integrated Mission Statements® defined, written out, signed, (if possible) by appropriate participating individuals, and posted for all to see, reference, and use as a benchmark for their conversations, agendas, and actions.

4. The Ritz Carlton premium hotel chain states in their mission statement that they are "ladies and gentlemen serving ladies and gentlemen." That is a very clear mission directive to guide your actions and non-actions. What does your mission statement indicate?

5. An easy template for crafting your mission statement at any of the five levels is to write on a piece of paper or Word Document, Vertically along the left hand side, each of the letters below, followed by a dash. Then write after each letter, powerful descriptive words for who you are (or your company / organization is) and what you do. Now, take that sequence of words, and craft them into a coherent, fluid sentence.

W - _____

W - _____

W - _____

W - _____

W - _____

H - _____

Any well-written mission statement should be able to be benchmarked from these six letters.

6. Make a note to remind yourself to review these five guideposts on a quarterly basis in order to make sure all Human Capital assets are aligned, and that you are continuously in alignment with market needs.

7. Go to www.jeffreymagee.com and sign up for the weekly Performance Execution email newsletter for access to a series of articles on the power of mission statements, which also include helpful tips for designing and implementing effective mission statements.

8. Practical Application – Identify a fifth Performance Execution accountability plan of action that you can design and commit to implementing, that will bring this chapter to life for you.

_____

_____

_____

_____

_____

_____

_____

_____

_____

_____

_____

_____

1. Identify any decision you are contemplating right now, big or small, and reflect on that subject matter. Follow the four-step decision model to see how your mind has been pre-conditioned to work. Can you easily move from the S step through to the P step, or do you find yourself mentally slowed down or stopped at any step? If you see what your present decision style looks like, then you can start to see how you may approach any, and every decision.

2. Performance Execution is about making sure you spend the least amount of time on the first two steps, and the most time on the third step. In the final analysis, you must get to the fourth and final step in a judicious amount of time!

3. Go to *www.jeffreymagee.com* for access to a series of articles on decision-making, gaining buy-in, and implementation success.

4. Consider posting a STOP sign next to your desk, in your day planner, on your walls at work, and in the rooms frequently used for meetings, as a guidepost to avoid getting bogged down in repetitive discussions around step one. Make sure you make the case at step two, and ensure you and others spend quality time at step three!

5. Practical Application – Identify a sixth Performance Execution accountability plan of action that you can design and commit to implementing, that will bring this chapter to life for you.

_____

_____

_____

_____

_____

_____

_____

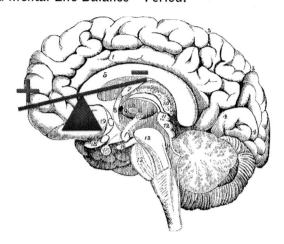

1. Go to *www.ThePerformanceMagazine.com* and sign up for electronic
performance articles and updates from the leading Performance Execution
personalities of our time! Each week, when you receive them in your e-mail box,
create an electronic file folder and save them, so you can act upon them later.

2. Go to *www.JeffreyMagee.com* and sign up for the weekly electronic
performance article and updates. Each week, when you receive them in your
e-mail box, create an electronic file folder and save them, so you can and act
upon them.

3. Take a piece of paper and reflect upon what you were doing professionally
ten years ago. With that reference point, consider who was in your life then,
who is no longer occupying mental teeter-totter space today. Is that a good or
bad thing? Can you see how the void of that person plays on your psyche and
Performance Execution level?

4. As you interact with the next person (professionally or personally) that you
may not know very well, ask questions to find out about the influences within
them as they relate to the individual PFC FISHES categories. The more you
know about someone, the greater your opportunity will be for effective and non-
combative engagement with them.

5. Consider the Ladder of Life metaphor. Whoever you are, place yourself
on a ladder rung near the bottom. Consider the ladder to be representative of

anything you aspire to do, be, or accomplish. On that ladder, identify and place onto it those people who are before you, above you, better than you, and more accomplished than you on the same ladder you are climbing. Also recognize who would be immediately behind you or below you. You are never the top rung in this equation. With this model in mind, let it represent one of your goals or aspirations. Take a piece of paper or create an Excel spreadsheet and write down ten people who would be above you on this ladder. With those names as a target, explore how to go about meeting each one. Imagine what your performance teeter-totter would look like if those people were placed onto your actual Ladder of Life.

6. Practical Application – Identify a seventh Performance Execution accountability plan of action that you can design and commit to implementing, that will bring this chapter to life for you.

_____

_____

_____

_____

_____

_____

_____

_____

_____

_____

Practical Application Tool Kit Activities
Conclusion: Stand Up, Shut Up & Take Ownership

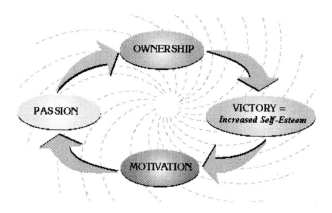

1. Starting with VICTORY, identify a personal mega accomplishment or victory that you have experienced in recent times. With that reference point, replay in your head that experience, how you felt, how it energized or re-MOTIVATED you, and what it did for your PASSION. In turn, what did that do to cause you to assume more or less ownership of the endeavor that started the cycle?

2. Take your time management system (PDA, Outlook, PALM, Blackberry, DayTimer, etc.) and log an action item or task on at east one day each week for the next two months. Choose an action that you know plays to your strengths, and that you know would be an instant VICTORY for you. With that action task or item logged into your system, make sure you have that VICTORY each week and chronicle that experience.

3. Inventory the last few awards, accolades, and citations you've received for any true VICTORY you attained. From these, recognize if those VICTORIES brought you satisfaction and MOTIVATED you, and if that drove your PASSION and caused you to assume greater control, responsibility, or OWNERSHIP of the endeavor. If so, let those serve as the reference points to what your X-Factor may be, and then apply these Performance Execution technologies to it for even greater success and VIP stature!

4. Practical Application – Identify an eighth Performance Execution accountability plan of action that you can design and commit to implementing, that will bring this chapter to life for you.

_____

_____

_____

_____

_____

_____

_____

_____

_____

_____

Practical Application Tool Kit Activities
Appendix One: Working the Generational Diversity Gap Will Be Your Organizational Asset

1. HOLLYWOOD GETS IT - Attend one movie per week for the next five weeks. Choose movies which are targeted to different generational segmentations. Arrive at a major movie house at least 30 minutes prior to the actual movie. Take note of the people, conversations, the pre-movie on-screen vignettes, movie trailers, video disc jockeys and their commentary, clothes, dress, music, commercials, etc. What you will recognize by the fourth generational segmentation experience is that Hollywood understands how to connect with each generational segmentation on their own level. Take note, you can learn from them. Notice the subtle differences used in advertising, marketing, and communicating to each different generational segmentation.

2. Starbucks lobby time. Spend a few hours at your local Starbucks and observe how each generational segmentation actually patronizes the store. How does each act in the store, dress, buy, and experience the Starbucks environment? Notice the generational diversity of workers and customers, and how each interacts when they have a common connection?

3. Create the inverted L-Grid model (referenced earlier in Appendix One) and ask those around you to describe their views of you as it pertains to the ABC MAPS model. Remember, perception is king. Recognize how they expect you to act, and ways to enhance and change their perception for greater Performance Execution.

4. Do this same drill with those with whom you live, work, and socialize. Learn how to adjust your interactions with them for greater Performance Execution in the future.

5. To ensure your fluid understanding of how each generational segmentation may operate with some similar, and some distinct differences, create a list of how each may have been influenced by technology in their life. For example, associate each of these telephone technology evolutions with the appropriate generational segmentation: Party Line v. Rotary Line v. Cordless Line v. Cell Phone v. Personal Delivery Vehicle multi-purpose device (phone, internet, podcast, database, gaming system, etc.).

6. Practical Application – Identify an ninth Performance Execution accountability plan of action that you can design and commit to implementing, that will bring this chapter to life for you.

_____

_____

_____

_____

_____

_____

_____

_____

_____

Practical Application Tool Kit Activities

Appendix Two: Awakening the Leadership Potentials Within You and Others...

Putting Performance Execution to Work with the "Control" and "Entrepreneurial" Forces Within You and Your Organization (cForce® v. eForce®)

1. Self-observation evaluation questions: Is the position that you professionally serve within a cForce or an eForce position? Is your overall professional personality that of a cForce or eForce person? Do you see how these observations impact your Performance Execution and what accountability safeguards you may want to employ to ensure you attain Performance Execution from your core X-Factor abilities?

2. Organizational observation questions: Evaluate every position (on a sheet of paper) that your employer presently has and identify whether they are cForce or eForce positions within your organization. Now personally identify the actual person in each position and identify whether that person is a cForce or eForce person. Do you see how these observations impact the Performance Execution of your organization? If there are any misalignments, what accountability safeguards may you want to employ to ensure your organization does not implode?

3. Apply this model to your elected local, state, and federal politicians to determine for what position you need to cast your ballot, and have someone represent you. Then ask yourself what personality the person you are about to vote for has. Given these two answers, if you mis-elect, then you should not be upset if they misbehave.

4. Practical Application – Identify a tenth Performance Execution accountability plan of action that you can design and commit to implementing, that will bring this chapter to life for you.

_____

_____

_____

_____

_____

_____

_____

Practical Application Tool Kit Activities
Appendix Three: Building Respectful Interactive RELATIONSHIPS with Others...
The Four Core Building Blocks to Performance Execution with Another Person

1. Mentally identify a performance implosion among two other people in your personal or professional life that is either taking place right now, or took place in recent history. With that implosion in mind, can you see which Relationship Cube® withdrawals, or lack of deposits compounded that implosion?

2. Think of someone new in your life right now. If you were to create an inventory of the four sides to the Relationship Cube as it pertains to them, would you know what a dozen deposits would be for each side? These are, in essence, their valuable teeter-totter deposits.

3. Practical Application – Identify an eleventh Performance Execution accountability plan of action that you can design and commit to implementing, that will bring this chapter to life for you.

_____

_____

_____

_____

_____

_____

_____

_____

_____

_____

Practical Application Tool Kit Activities
Appendix Four: What Do You Do to Not "SUC" Right Now?

1. Take your personal time management system (PDA, Outlook, Palm, Blackberry, DayPlanner, desk or wall calendar, etc.) and log a reminder note at the beginning of each month for the next twelve months to review what you did during the previous year. This will drive your negative teeter-totter influences crazy, as you hold them accountable for forward success behaviors through Performance Execution success reminders!

2. Share the list with your performance coach or an accountability partner!

3. Reflect upon the trade industry you are a part of now, and find one significant conference, meeting, event, symposium, or rally to attend each quarter. Sign up now, pay your admittance fees now, and make the hotel and/or airline reservations now, as a sign of accountability and commitment to your own PQ goals.

4. Do the same if you aspire to a different trade industry than the one in which you are presently living and working. Find one significant conference, meeting, event, symposium, or rally to attend each quarter that will serve you in better understanding and transitioning into your new career direction. Sign up now, pay your admittance fees now, and make the hotel and/or airline reservations now, as a sign of accountability and commitment to your own PQ goals.

5. Practical Application – Identify a twelfth Performance Execution accountability plan of action that you can design and commit to implementing, that will bring this chapter to life for you.

_____

_____

_____

_____

_____

_____

_____

_____

_____

_____

_____

Free Bonus Offer

Free Weekly Performance Execution Electronic Success Column Delivered to Your E-mail Address and Other Performance Execution Offers – Gain a Strategic Advantage in the Marketplace Now!

As a reader of *Performance Execution* you can receive a FREE one-year subscription to Jeff Magee's Performance Execution eZine, delivered directly to your personal e-mail box every week. Each week you will receive a powerful how-to oriented column in an easy to read, 500-word, one-page format. You will never read commentary, trends, or a feature on anyone. Always, and only, actionable content you can use right now to attain Performance Execution greatness!

Subscribe now and collect the entire year's columns to have more than 52 weeks of action-packed Performance Execution-oriented mental tools.

Go to *www.JeffreyMagee.com* and subscribe to the Performance Execution leadership weekly column today!

Share the performance power with your family, friends, and colleagues by signing them up as well! Refer them to *www.JeffreyMagee.com*!

Other powerful self-development options for you:

1. *www.ThePerformanceMagazine.com* Subscribe to Performance Magazine and receive a special bonus - 20+ regional editions of ***Professional Performance Magazine*** featuring hundreds of local performance stars sharing their personal secrets for success!

2. *www.ThePerformanceMagazine.com* Sign up for a special COMPLIMENTARY three-month GOLD membership in the Performance KnowledgeVault featuring powerful personal and professional Performance Execution add-ons to your VIP stature!

3. Visit *www.performancelivetv.com* to access several powerful interviews between Dr. Jeff Magee and business & civic leaders. Performance television at its most impactful!

4. Contact the author directly at *Jeff@JeffreyMagee.com* to learn more about his 52 weeks to PERFORMANCE EXECUTION SUCCESS Coaching Program!

About the Author

J eff Magee has been called one of the leading "Leadership & Marketing Strategists" today. Jeff started his first business at age 15, and sold it before going to college. Before the age of 21, he had penned more than 100 newspaper columns appearing in major daily newspapers. By age 24, he was recognized by American Home Products, a Fortune 500 company, as one of their top salesmen in the nation, while at the same time becoming the youngest certified Sales Instructor in the World, for the Dale Carnegie Sales Course. After experiencing downsizing in 1987, Jeff went on to work as a sales associate for the nation's largest educational and youth advertising/marketing firm, Target Marketing, and was promoted to Vice President of Sales and Chief Operating Officer, within two years!

For the past twenty-one years Jeff has lead the team at Jeff Magee International / JMI, Inc., as one of the industry's leading human capital talent management and development niche firms. As a tax-payer, payroll-provider, and employer, he has learned that theories are good, but it is the practicum and reality that pays the bills.

As a performance execution Coach, Jeff is well-credentialed. He is a Certified Speaking Professional (CSP), a Certified Management Consultant (CMC) and a Certified Professional Direct Marketer (PDM), and has been recognized as one of the "Ten Outstanding Young Americans" (known as TOYA) by the United States Junior Chamber of Commerce. Jeff is a three-term President of the Oklahoma Speakers Association, and was twice awarded their Professional Speaker Member of the Year. Today, the Chapter's outstanding member of the year is awarded the "Jeff Magee Member of the Year Award"!

For years, Jeff has participated in awarding an annual scholarship to an emerging professional Member of the Oklahoma Speakers Association Chapter – "The Magee-Stovall High Impact Emerging Speaker Award" – and has an endowed Scholarship at his undergraduate alma mater, Baker University in Baldwin City, Kansas.

Today, Jeff is the writer of a national leadership column (which you may have seen in your own local newspaper) and serves as the Publisher of the national success publication series, *Professional Performance Magazine (www. ThePerformanceMagazine.com)* with more than 30 National, International, and Affinity Publisher editions.

Jeff is the author of more than 20 books, transcribed into multiple languages, including 4 Best-Sellers. His dissertation was converted into the text, *Yield Management* and was the #1 selling graduate management school textbook in 2000 for CRC/St. Lucie Press. His 2008 release of *It: Find It, Get It, Keep It, Grow It*, an innovative turn-key approach to selling, expanded his 2004 work in the McGraw-Hill best-selling *The Sales Training Handbook* for performance execution among sales professionals and military recruiters nationally - a favorite of success-oriented individuals.

Go to www.JeffreyMagee.com, www.amazon.com, or www.BarnesNoble.com to obtain all of his available books, audios, and downloadable videos, for your self-development library today.

Along with being recognized as the longest-running invited featured lecturer for the Boeing Leadership Institute, many Fortune 500 firms (including Harley-Davidson, Anheuser-Busch, USA/NASA, and El Paso Energy) use Jeff for PERFORMANCE EXECUTION® in the areas of managerial-leadership effectiveness and sales training and coaching. Jeff has been repeatedly invited to share performance ideas with leading "think-tanks" like the Conference Board (the Diversity Council and Human Resources Council), College Board, and Boomer CPA Consulting Circles. He has been the keynote speaker for many major associations, including: ABA, AICPA, Farm Credit Services, NSA, MPI, and ASTD across America. Jeff has also been invited to speak at West Point Military Academy and the National Guard on the subject of leadership!

In 2001, Jeff was commissioned to design, present a series of national leadership and sales recruitment programs for more than 5,000 professional sales recruiters and sales managers with the U.S. Army National Guard. As a result of this, he subsequently received the prestigious Commander's Coins of Excellence!

Powerful (public) human capital training seminar firms like CareerTrack Seminars and SkillPath Seminars have asked Jeff to design many of the skill development classes they have provided over the past two decades, including the design and narration of some of their top-selling self-development training videos, DVDs, and audio programs.

In 2007, Tulsa Oklahoma Mayor Kathy Taylor (D) appointed Jeff to a five-year term as a Commissioner for the City of Tulsa's Civil Service Commission (CSC). The CSC serves as the final authority for any civil service personnel and human resources policy issues, endeavors, or grievances, and serves as the supervisory body for the City of Tulsa Personnel Director.

The London Business Gazette has hailed Jeff as "an American business guru." The Chamber of Commerce in Jeff's hometown of Tulsa, Oklahoma awarded him the Small Business Administrations Business Publisher of the Year Award in 2008-2009, and the State of Oklahoma Small Business Association did the same in 2009. The United States Army National Guard and Former President George W. Bush recognized him with the high honor of the "National Guard Total Victory Team" medal, for his service to the U.S. National Guard.

To Book Jeff...

Jeff can be scheduled for your next Conference, Convention, Retreat, or for an on-site, high-impact, results-driven development program by contacting:

Info@JeffreyMagee.com
or by calling
Toll free 1-877-90-MAGEE

MANAGERIAL-LEADERSHIP & SALES TRAINING WITHOUT LIMITS

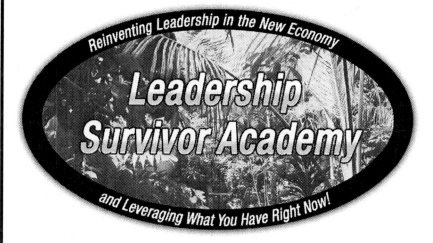

Dr. Jeff Magee has developed a Leadership training series like nothing before, personalized to your organization.

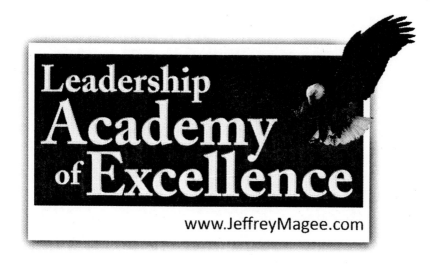

Leadership Academy Of Excellence is only for the serious leader-driven organization. The Fundamentals of **Managerial-Leadership Effectiveness** focuses on the strategic aspects of transformational Managerial-Leadership skills for leaders, directors and managers of today's top business and sales organizations; what you must possess to engage, grow, support, challenge and prepare succession planning.

This year-long executive development program combines face-to-face consulting and presentations, with on-demand digital tools and resources, and has been designed out of our proven work with the Fortune 100 corporations, the largest national membership-driven associations, and the top military National Guard Adjutant Generals in America. The content, which will be customized to meet your company's specific needs, is extracted from our bestselling books, and based on sales organizational research and certification work.

Imagine the power, impact AND results that this program can deliver with continual success-oriented performance and follow-up deliverables for each module!
Find out more at www.jeffreymagee.com